Authors · Paris Crenshaw, Jim Groves, Sean McGowen, and Philip Minchin

Cover Artist · Claudia Schmidt
Interior Artists · Donald Crank, Ian Llanas, Derek Murphy, Chenthooran Nambiarooran, Andy Timm, Lindsey Wakefield, and Vicky Yarova

Creative Director · James Jacobs
Editor-in-Chief · F. Wesley Schneider
Managing Editor · James L. Sutter
Lead Developer · Patrick Renie

Senior Developer · Rob McCreary
Developers · Logan Bonner, John Compton, Adam Daigle, Mark Moreland, Patrick Renie, and Owen K.C. Stephens
Associate Editors · Judy Bauer and Christopher Carey
Editors · Justin Juan, Ryan Macklin, and Matthew Simmons
Lead Designer · Jason Bulmahn
Designer · Stephen Radney-MacFarland

Managing Art Director · Sarah E. Robinson
Senior Art Director · Andrew Vallas
Art Director · Sonja Morris
Graphic Designers · Emily Crowell and Ben Mouch

Publisher · Erik Mona
Paizo CEO · Lisa Stevens
Chief Operations Officer · Jeffrey Alvarez
Director of Sales · Pierce Watters
Sales Associate · Cosmo Eisele
Marketing Director · Jenny Bendel
Finance Manager · Christopher Self
Staff Accountant · Ashley Gillaspie
Chief Technical Officer · Vic Wertz
Senior Software Developer · Gary Teter
Campaign Coordinator · Mike Brock
Project Manager · Jessica Price
Licensing Coordinator · Michael Kenway

Customer Service Team · Erik Keith, Sharaya Kemp, Katina Mathieson, and Sara Marie Teter
Warehouse Team · Will Chase, Mika Hawkins, Heather Payne, Jeff Strand, and Kevin Underwood
Website Team · Christopher Anthony, Liz Courts, Crystal Frasier, Lissa Guillet, and Chris Lambertz

ON THE COVER

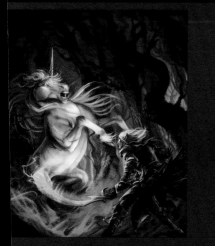

This righteous unicorn is no match for black-hearted Seltyiel, and this month's cover illustration by Claudia Schmidt proves it.

TABLE OF CONTENTS

REFERENCE

This Pathfinder Player Companion refers to several other Pathfinder Roleplaying Game products and uses the following abbreviations. These books are not required to make use of this Player Companion. Readers interested in references to Pathfinder RPG hardcovers can find the complete rules from these books available for free at **paizo.com/prd**.

Advanced Player's Guide	APG	*Bestiary 3*	B4
Advanced Race Guide	ARG	*Ultimate Combat*	UC
Bestiary 2	B2	*Ultimate Magic*	UM
Bestiary 3	B3		

Paizo Inc.
7120 185th Ave NE, Ste 120
Redmond, WA 98052-0577

paizo.com

This product is compliant with the Open Game License (OGL) and is suitable for use with the Pathfinder Roleplaying Game or the 3.5 edition of the world's oldest fantasy roleplaying game.

Product Identity: The following items are hereby identified as Product Identity, as defined in the Open Game License version 1.0a, Section 1(e), and are not Open Content: All trademarks, registered trademarks, proper names (characters, deities, etc.), dialogue, plots, storylines, locations, characters, artwork, and trade dress. (Elements that have previously been designated as Open Game Content or are in the public domain are not included in this declaration.)

Open Content: Except for material designated as Product Identity (see above), the game mechanics of this Paizo game product are Open Game Content, as defined in the Open Gaming License version 1.0a Section 1(d). No portion of this work other than the material designated as Open Game Content may be reproduced in any form without written permission.

Pathfinder Player Companion: Champions of Corruption © 2014, Paizo Inc. All Rights Reserved. Paizo, Paizo Inc., the Paizo golem logo, Pathfinder, the Pathfinder logo, and Pathfinder Society are registered trademarks of Paizo Inc.; Pathfinder Accessories, Pathfinder Adventure Card Game, Pathfinder Adventure Path, Pathfinder Campaign Setting, Pathfinder Cards, Pathfinder Flip-Mat, Pathfinder Map Pack, Pathfinder Module, Pathfinder Pawns, Pathfinder Player Companion, Pathfinder Roleplaying Game, and Pathfinder Tales are trademarks of Paizo Inc.

Printed in the U.S.A.

FOR YOUR CHARACTER

FOCUS CHARACTERS

This Pathfinder Player Companion highlights new options specific to characters of the following classes, as well as elements that apply to a wide range of characters.

Antipaladins

No class embodies the might and determination of wickedness as much as the antipaladin. The dread vanguard archetype (page 22) provides antipaladins a way of showcasing the powers of evil without necessarily devoting themselves to a particular deity or otherworldly force of darkness.

Clerics

The inside front cover and page 18 provide complete details for worshipers of some of Golarion's most prominent evil deities. New cleric subdomains on pages 18–19 provide dastardly priests new means of executing their unholy patrons' wills, and are also available to other classes capable of gaining subdomains (such as druids and inquisitors).

Fighters

A host of vile new feats are the fighter's greatest arsenal throughout this volume. In addition to a handful of combat feats that make smashing objects as useful as it is fun (see page 23), teamwork feats and combat traits (see the facing page) round out the evil fighter's arsenal of rules options.

Summoners

Channel the powers of blood into your eidolon like the corrupted god-callers of the Worldwound with the new blood summoner archetype on page 24. Summoners and any other spellcasters who take pleasure in unleashing the armies of Hell or the hordes of the Abyss upon their enemies will also be well served by the new Summon Evil Monster feat and the *summon monster* list on the back inside cover.

FOR EVERY CHARACTER

Certain game concepts transcend the particulars of a character's race or class. The following elements detailed in this book work equally well for any character you want to play in the Pathfinder Roleplaying Game, regardless of the character's background, focus, or type.

Motivations

Most evil isn't inspired solely by a desire for chaos or the thrill of meaningless violence (though those are certainly aspects of it). True evil-doers have other motives as well, and the suggestions on pages 4–5 provide inspiration for countless vile and despicable characters. Whether you embrace dark teachings to fulfill quests for magical power or you hope to enact vengeance on the do-gooders who betrayed you long ago, the motives behind your evil campaign are as important as the cruel deeds you enact.

Evil Alignments

On pages 6–11, three articles on the different faces of evil as depicted by the alignments lawful evil, neutral evil, and chaotic evil provide ample opportunity for you to develop a character as compelling as she is corrupt. In addition to detailed analyses and discussions of the challenges and advantages inherent to each evil alignment, every alignment section includes sample personality archetypes to try for your evil characters, examples of the types of organizations on Golarion your villain may be drawn to, and new character traits specifically designed for evil characters.

QUESTIONS TO ASK YOUR GM

Asking your GM the following questions can help you get the most out of *Pathfinder Player Companion: Champions of Corruption.*

1 Is it okay for my character to have a lawful evil, neutral evil, or chaotic evil alignment?

2 Should the entire party be evil, or is it okay to have a mix of good, neutral, and evil characters at the table? Is player-versus-player combat allowed?

3 Is our campaign designed specifically for evil characters? Will being evil significantly hinder or benefit me in any way?

Damnation

Some villains go to great lengths to garner power over evil. Are you one of them? All-new rules for selling your eternal soul to a fiendish deity in return for unholy strength make their debut in this book in the form of the damnation feats on pages 16–17.

Cooperating with Evil

Playing an evil character presents interesting dilemmas not normally encountered in groups of neutral or good adventurers. The sidebars on pages 5–11 detail some of the implications of playing evil characters, and provide advice and material for discussion so you and your group can ensure alignment disputes don't get in the way of a good time.

DID YOU KNOW?
Alignment arguments are a time-honored tradition in roleplaying games—even within the Paizo offices! For example, Creative Director James Jacobs and Managing Editor James L. Sutter have a long-standing debate on the actual alignment of Mengkare, the gold dragon that Sutter created to run the morally ambiguous human-breeding experiment in Hermea. To this day, Paizo has never officially declared whether Mengkare is good, neutral, or evil...

RULES INDEX

The following new rules options are located on the indicated pages throughout this book.

WHY BE EVIL?

Evil lurks in every corner of Golarion. An imprisoned god of destruction rages at its core. Cruelty and madness bubble through its subterranean vaults. The planet's surface is scarred by an Abyssal eruption, and nations ruled by devils, monsters, torture cults, undead, and evil witch clans stain the land. Beyond Golarion, evil entities dominate significant portions of the Outer Planes, and the implacable, inscrutable forces of the Dark Tapestry stare down from between the stars. It's no wonder that players might want to explore Golarion's shadows—they provide rich fodder for adventures.

REASONS FOR EVIL

Outside of fables and morality plays, crime and ruthlessness often pay quite well, and life on Golarion is not exempt from this sad reality. Yet in a world where divine judgment is inevitable and magic lets the living glimpse places like Hell, Abaddon, and the Abyss for themselves, there are plenty of reasons to renounce evil and walk the path of righteousness. So why make enemies in this world and damn yourself in the afterlife? The following questions can help inform an evil background.

- Is your life of evil a conscious choice, or the result of never considering the effects of your actions on others?
- Are you simply reflecting the values of the culture in which you were raised? Did your upbringing give you a skewed view of right and wrong?
- Do you believe that the end justifies the means, and that your noble objectives will eventually offset your monstrous deeds?
- Do you see yourself as being not evil, but instead simply driven? Do you justify your actions by saying that you don't like hurting people, but you want what you want, and you'll crawl over the bodies of whoever stands in your way to get it?
- Did a traumatic event or abusive childhood leave you hurt, unable to empathize, or prone to taking out your rage on others?
- Do you believe you can avoid or transcend all the consequences of your actions? Do you plan somehow to circumvent divine judgment, perhaps through your own undeath?
- Are you convinced that evil, or a particular evil force or being, will eventually triumph over good? If so, are you aligning yourself with it out of ambition, or simply to survive?
- Does evil offer you something you believe you can't get any other way?
- Are you convinced evil is your inescapable nature—or perhaps reality's—and thus not worth fighting against?
- Will you be evil only until something awakens your inner hero? (If so, what might that trigger be, and why are you currently evil instead of simply neutral?)
- Are you evil simply for the fun of it?

MOTIVATIONS FOR EVIL CHARACTERS

One way to develop evil characters is to examine their motivations. Below are some underlying motivations for adopting an evil alignment, and some questions your character may face in the course of play.

Appetite: Driven by curiosity, obsession, neurosis, or the search for pleasure, your desire for certain experiences or possessions lies outside the bounds of so-called morality. Maybe the first taboos you broke were minor, but your inner urges push you to ever more extreme violations. Costs mount, and sometimes tastes change—how much can your appetite endure?

Despair: You see yourself as a realist. You wish things could be better, but they can't. Hope is a cruel illusion, and the kindest thing you can do for everyone (including yourself) is to shatter that illusion whenever it appears. Given such a grim outlook, what keeps you going?

Entitlement: You're special. Reality rightly bends around your desires. When people tell you otherwise, you either crush them and put them in their places, or persecute others to reassure yourself of your power. What makes you think you're so important? Could anything convince you otherwise?

Expedience: You can see how playing by the rules could be nice, but it's so complicated and restrictive! You just take the simplest path to your goal no matter who or what is in the way. If that makes you a monster, so be it.

Ignorance: You commit horrific acts because you genuinely don't know better. Either you were raised to adhere to a set of monstrous values, or something in your past left you unable to empathize with others (or with creatures of a certain group). Is this willful ignorance? What could change you?

Need: For some reason, you cannot survive without sinning. Perhaps you have succumbed to lycanthropy or vampirism, or have become so addicted to something that you'll do anything to get more. How much evil does lack of choice excuse? How much of your need is real, and how much is all in your head?

Power: You love power for its own sake, and any attempt to bind you with morality is an unreasonable burden. What will you do when you encounter a foe you cannot defeat?

Purpose: Your mission might not be inherently evil—it might even be noble—but it's too important to compromise. If atrocities will get the job done, you don't hesitate. But are you sinning to serve your purpose, or are you drawn to your purpose because it gives you license to sin?

Rage: Maybe the world hurt you, and now you hurt it. Maybe this wrath is focused on particular groups, maybe particular groups are exempt from a general hatred, or maybe you just hate indiscriminately. Is there some final vengeance or absolution that could quench your fire?

Terror: Something scares you, and you'll do anything to escape it. Fear of death might drive you toward undeath. Fear of powerful forces might trigger blind obedience, frantic attempts at appeasement, or Pyrrhic victories. Can you ever truly escape your fear?

MAKING EVIL FUN

The great gift of roleplaying is that it allows people to temporarily experience what it's like to be someone else, and sometimes it can be fun play someone very different from yourself—a person who may transgress your own morals and taboos. Playing an evil character can be a safe and entertaining way to explore humanity's darker urges, as well as a way to help us better understand the motives and basic personhood of those people we might otherwise write off as simply "bad."

Yet while playing an evil character can be rewarding, it's also challenging. As a member of an adventuring party, an evil character may see other characters as adversaries, victims, or expendable resources. That same selfish, potentially abusive mentality between players can ruin games, or even friendships.

The key to playing evil well is making sure everyone in your group is on the same page. While not every party member needs to be evil, every player does need to be comfortable with both where the story may go and the potential interpersonal dynamics. Just as there's nothing wrong with wanting to play an evil character, there's nothing wrong with *not* wanting to play that way, either. Above all, be honest and open—a conversation where people feel judged or pressured will only set your group up for failure.

First, your group should create guidelines for player interaction. For some groups, PC versus PC scheming, in-character insult battles, and even PCs literally backstabbing other PCs can be as much fun as working together against a challenge. Other groups feel the team bond is central to play, or just don't like interpersonal conflict in their leisure time; the line between attacking a PC and antagonizing the player can be hard to find, so talk about it up front.

Regardless of your play style, things will run smoother if you determine from the outset why the group works together. If you're the only evil character in a party, decide why your particular brand of evil makes you a good fit. Your party's paladin might take pity on a dangerous addict or tolerate a power-hungry noble if she's working toward the same goal as you are, but she probably can't work with someone who kills innocents for fun.

Perhaps most importantly, both your group and your GM need to agree on basic boundaries. Many people may have triggers, or situations that they absolutely don't want to come up in a game—examples might include rape or cruelty to children or animals. If someone voices such a concern, there should be no discussion—just leave those situations out of the game. Other things might be okay if they take place off-camera: a player could be fine with the story of torturing an enemy for information, but might not want to roleplay every grisly detail.

It's best to discuss these boundaries at the beginning, but bear in mind that comfort levels vary from person to person, and may change over time. If you or someone else stops enjoying the game, pause the action and adjust accordingly. And whatever guidelines your group agrees to, respect them—and each other.

LAWFUL EVIL

Lawful evil characters believe that law and structure mean power and safety. In their view, a strict, systematic hierarchy enables outcomes impossible for a single individual, so they seek power and security by positioning themselves advantageously within such systems. They may operate according to strict personal codes—private ethics or creeds that may not align with an observer's concept of morality—but more often choose to operate within (and take advantage of) the framework of the society around them. Many are quick to cite their law-abiding natures when defending their actions. This alignment is particularly appealing to those who want to get ahead and don't care whom they hurt, yet who also want to maintain a sense of self-righteousness or don't want to open themselves up to unnecessary risk. They may take great pride in never breaking their word—and thus rarely make promises—and are invariably methodical and organized in their machinations.

PHILOSOPHIES

Lawful evil characters appear on every rung of the social ladder. Some seek desperately to climb the ladder, dreaming of doing unto others what has been done to them. Others feel smug superiority toward the less fortunate and enjoy abusing their power and privilege. Following are some common lawful evil personality archetypes.

Despots

Destined to rule—at least in their own minds—despots seek to impose their will on those around them. Obedience is often not enough; a despot requires total submission. Despots are capable of collaboration and even subordination within a larger structure, but they usually get resentful if they don't climb the ranks quickly enough, and they seek out opportunities to give orders instead of taking them. Rarely, despots actually enjoy sharing power with like-minded souls; more often, their alliances are of convenience, and a pact's stability depends on whether the despot's goals are being met. While all despots believe themselves to be great leaders, not all are; dark tragicomedy abounds when incompetent despots achieve even a small measure of power.

If you are a despot, you:

- Demand blind obedience and servility.
- Welcome neither questions nor failures from your underlings.
- Constantly seek to expand your personal power base.

Code: Your commands are law—and woe betide those who disobey.

Minions

The world is a dangerous and confusing place, filled with overwhelmingly powerful entities. Thankfully, sometimes those beings take lucky souls under their wings, offering protection, purpose, and perhaps permission to indulge aspects of oneself that society otherwise prohibits. Whether the patron is a god, monster, nation, or mortal, the minion knows that loyalty and perfect service—no matter how distasteful or depraved the command—are the best ways to rise in the ranks and achieve comfort and security. Minions may take pride in their service or comfort in the fact that any responsibility for their actions ultimately lies with their masters. Total devotion is a small price to pay for the gifts these dark masters offer.

If you are a minion, you:

- Seek powerful figures to serve and obey.
- Avoid anything that might raise questions about your loyalty.
- Live to please your master, regardless of the harm to yourself or anyone else.

Code: Be an obedient and useful servant, and your master will take care of you.

Swindlers

Swindlers accumulate power through indirect means. By using deception and manipulation, and by exploiting the systems they inhabit, they gain personal advantage. Their most common method is brokering deals and contracts that seek to extract the maximum commitment from others while giving as little away as possible themselves. While driving a hard bargain is not itself evil, swindlers specifically prey on those at their most vulnerable, abusing the legal system and doing their best to exploit (or create) weakness. Loopholes and plausible deniability are a swindler's bread and butter, and most have legitimate business concerns to augment their extortion and entrapment. Often charming, always cunning, swindlers are experts at using people's own desires against them.

If you are a swindler, you:

- Look for exploits, loopholes, and advantages in every interaction and institution.
- Rarely break the law—working around it is so much more elegant.
- Are exceptionally proud of your wits and cunning.

Code: Anyone who shows weakness deserves to have it exploited.

ADVANTAGES AND CHALLENGES

Lawful evil characters are often surprisingly good at working with others, as long as doing so suits their agenda. Their organized minds excel at spotting ways to make a situation work for them, and they usually recognize that most systems require give and take between the various components. They tend to honor at least the letter of their agreements, and many lawful evil characters are capable of a cold self-discipline that lets them rein in unproductive traits when necessary.

At the same time, lawful evil characters who see weakness in their companions are often quick to capitalize on it, making them potential liabilities in combat. They may be unwilling to risk themselves for a cause or partner, or to bend to group decisions if they feel doing so places them at a disadvantage. Self-interest is the driving force for most lawful evil characters—even minions.

OPPORTUNITIES AND ALLIES

Lawful classes like the monk, samurai, and cavalier all have evil members, but perhaps the class most suited to lawful evil is the cleric, as both Asmodeus and Zon-Kuthon have powerful, hierarchical churches that provide lawful evil clerics with great opportunities. A witch's relationship to her patron and familiar and a summoner's to his eidolon can take on similar overtones at a smaller scale. Unethical wizards are also often drawn to lawful evil—the intellectual rigor of complex studies meshes well with a lawful disposition, and their pursuit of knowledge may lure them into deviant experimentation. And of course, while many people think of rogues as freewheeling criminals, some of the most effective masterminds and string-pullers are rogues and bards who abuse the law without breaking it.

Potential lawful evil allies in the Inner Sea region include the following.

Lawful Evil Nations: Cheliax's House Thrune owes its power and authority to Asmodeus and his devils, and those of a similar mind-set can go far with House Thrune's

One risk of an evil campaign is that the characters' selfishness can erode the team bond. Yet selfishness can also help characters overcome their differences, even across alignments.

Lawful evil characters who operate in groups usually focus on mutual self-interest. To them, other characters are resources, and no tool should be discarded out of hand if it can still be of use. For instance, chaotic characters may be messy, indisciplined wretches, but if a lawful evil character can channel that scattered energy into something productive, everyone can benefit. Good characters may be sanctimonious or sentimental, but as long as the evil they're stomping out is an evil that stands in your way, you have every reason to help them. A wise lawful evil character doesn't care about motives, only outcomes. By properly framing decisions for your allies and knowing how to manipulate them, you can point them in a direction that aids your objectives. And in the end, a lawful evil character doesn't need to have a problem with other characters succeeding—as long as she succeeds the most.

help. The satellite nation of Nidal offers an even bitterer flavor of tyranny. Geb is not friendly to the living, but necromancers can find allies there. The false god Razmir's cult-nation is a lawful evil pyramid scheme on a colossal scale. In Tian Xia, the oni of Chu Ye and the hobgoblins of Kaoling might collaborate with outsiders whose goals overlap theirs.

Slavers: The slave trade is a natural home for those drawn to exercising power over others. Those willing to profit from an industry built on kidnapping, murder, and torture can make fortunes in places like Okeno or the Shackles.

Subjugators: The Hellknights offer opportunities for those willing to follow a code and use punitive force unstintingly on command. The Silent Enforcers might aid those whose objectives help keep Nidal under Zon-Kuthon's thumb. The Red Mantis are happy to kill for coin, provided doing so doesn't break their laws.

TRAITS

The following new traits suit a lawful evil alignment.

Detect Disobedience (Social): You have an uncanny ability to spot a mutiny brewing. You gain a +2 trait bonus on Sense Motive checks to detect when an underling is trying to hide something from you, and can attempt such checks instead of Perception checks to notice and react to a subordinate's surprise attack against you.

Punish Insurrection (Combat): You relish reminding people who's in charge. Against members of the same organization or hierarchy who formally answer to you, you gain a +1 trait bonus on attack and damage rolls. You also gain this bonus against members who have openly defied the authority or rules of that body, provided the infraction is serious enough that their standing is now less than yours.

NEUTRAL EVIL

Neutral evil characters care only for themselves, and do whatever they think they can get away with. They place no stock in the ability of laws or codes to protect them, and thus don't bother to follow them. At the same time, they're less spontaneous and prone to whimsy than chaotic evil characters. In some ways, neutral evil is the purest form of evil, unburdened by any other tropes or tendencies. Whether a neutral evil character has chosen to practice evil for its own sake or—more often—simply has no empathy for others, the result is the same: cold, unfeeling cruelty.

Those who care nothing for others or the pain they cause, or who strive toward such indifference, are drawn to this alignment.

PHILOSOPHIES

Neutral evil characters are not necessarily enthusiastic murderers—it's so messy and causes so much potential trouble—but they rarely have qualms with the deed itself. They are fundamentally interested only in themselves and their own dark desires and tastes. Other people are insects, tools, toys, or simply objects in their way.

Annihilists

Nothing matters. Entropy and chaos have created a world where nothing lasts, nothing means anything, and even the greatest works or truths will fall to dust and obscurity in the blink of an eye. You know that those who claim otherwise do themselves and everyone else a disservice, and you cannot abide anyone who perpetuates society's great lies of love and meaning. Instead, you choose to reveal their willful ignorance by furthering the cause of destruction. The world offends you, and thus you will bring it down.

If you are an annihilist, you:

- Have no feelings or scruples, or aspire to have none.
- See entropy and death everywhere, and accept (and inflict) them as the true pillars of reality.
- Despise anything that aspires to permanence, growth, or meaning.

Code: Everything crumbles. Who are you to argue with that?

Narcissists

Narcissists see meaning and beauty in the world—but only when they look in a mirror. For narcissists, the world truly does revolve around them: whatever makes them unhappy is a tragic injustice, and whatever pleases them is theirs by divine right. Narcissists can be genuinely bewildered—or homicidally enraged—by suggestions that anyone else's concerns take precedence over theirs. The narcissist differs from the lawful evil tyrant in that he has no particular need for power or authority, so long as all his whims are catered to without question. It's only when those whims are denied that the true, uncaring evil of the narcissist rears its bloody head.

If you are a narcissist, you:

- See everything in terms of its effect on you.

- Are surprised, shocked, or disgusted when the world or other people don't cater to your expectations.
- Are incapable of empathizing with others and can justify just about any horrific actions that serve your greater purpose.

Code: The universe knows what you want, so what does it expect when it doesn't it give it to you?

Psychopaths

Psychopaths are individuals who, for whatever reason, are unable to feel empathy and remorse, leading them to indulge in uninhibitedly antisocial behavior. A psychopath may or may not understand that others have feelings, but either way is unable to relate to other creatures. Other people are objects to them—sometimes amusing and sometimes useful, but always disposable.

If you are a psychopath, you:
- Never feel remorse or empathy.
- Indulge your whims in bold, often horrific ways.
- Know that all living things—even other people—are just objects.

Code: Do anything you want. Anything.

Advantages and Challenges

Neutral evil characters embody pure selfishness. That singleminded dedication to themselves typically makes their inner lives very straightforward. Many strongly neutral evil characters are emotionless and affectless, sometimes to a terrifying degree, which further focuses their mental resources on getting what they want, and can make them experts at whatever interests them. If their lack of inhibition manifests as admirable boldness and fearlessness, they may become master infiltrators and manipulators.

Opportunities and Allies

Almost any adventuring class can be neutral evil—killing people and taking their stuff is central to the job, and fewer scruples mean more opportunities. This is particularly true of rogues and ninjas, with their specialties in lying, sneaking, stealing, and backstabbing, but rangers, with their gift for patient predation and dedicated hate, and alchemists (especially poisoners) also make great choices for neutral evil characters.

Potential neutral evil allies on Golarion include the following forces.

Corrupt Governments: While neutral evil characters may not have the same drive for governmental power as their lawful evil counterparts, psychopaths' ability to manipulate others and operate boldly and without guilt often makes them quite adept at navigating the political system and using it to further their own ends.

Neutral Evil Organizations: The most prominent and widespread neutral evil organization in the Inner Sea region (though not always openly so) is the Aspis Consortium—unscrupulous merchants with a talent for making money at others' expense. The cult of undeath

NEUTRAL EVIL ALLIANCES

Provided neutral evil characters are getting what they want, they have no problem working with anyone else. They can even be trustworthy for extended periods of time when a larger goal is at stake or their interests or goals overlap with others'. If someone pleases them and seems nonthreatening, they may look after that person, possibly even becoming protective, though with a tendency toward possessiveness.

Neutral evil characters tend to project their own extreme selfishness onto others, which can be corrosive to trust. This selfishness and paranoia, plus the universal mortal tendency to be more conscious of one's own efforts than other people's, means that neutral evil characters can come to feel that a perfectly fair deal is in fact weighted against them. More intelligent neutral evil characters may be able to resist this cognitive bias, but it can be a serious impediment to long-term collaboration.

Neutral evil characters often work willingly with lawful evil or chaotic evil types, covertly regarding both the orderly and the wild with a slightly bemused condescension, except when these allies' behavior interferes with business. When working with neutral or good characters, neutral evil characters are generally careful to keep their vicious sides hidden except when necessary—or when they know they can get away with it.

known as the Whispering Way is also a draw for those without scruples. Thieves' guilds are often neutral evil, as they're too opportunistic and flexible to be lawful evil, yet too regimented to be truly chaotic evil.

Undead: Urgathoa, goddess of undeath, is neutral evil, and many of those who worship her—as well as most undead abominations themselves—share her alignment. More broadly, any necromancers or other spellcasters who care only for gaining hidden information or magical power, regardless of the potential cost to others, may be neutral evil.

Traits

The following traits suit a neutral evil alignment.

Horrifying Mind (Magic): When a nonevil humanoid attempts to read your mind via a magical effect, the reader must attempt a Will save opposed by your Wisdom or Charisma check (your choice). If the reader fails this save, she is shaken for 1 round. If she fails by 10 or more, she is instead frightened for 1 round, then shaken for 1 round.

Subjective Truth (Social): You are able to divorce your knowledge of the facts from your beliefs about the truth, and thus from your facial expressions and body language. You gain a +2 trait bonus on Bluff checks to lie, provided the person you're lying to has never known you to lie to him. Failing this check counts as being caught in a lie by the target, negating any future use of this bonus against that person.

CHAOTIC EVIL

Chaotic evil characters live at the mercy of their own toxic passions. Their goals and methods may change on a whim, and they often crave novelty and variety in their lives. While still capable of planning, they may have a hard time with patient, long-term scheming, preferring immediate satisfaction and direct action. For some, spreading chaos and destruction is a deliberate goal, yet more often chaotic evil characters are those who simply don't care whom their desires may hurt. They may see a certain nobility in their refusal to be bound by any conventions or creeds, or they may simply indulge their greed, hatred, and lust with no thought to the consequences. They may be emotionally or mentally unstable, letting their inner turmoil and turbulence spill out uncontrollably into others' lives. Yet, they need not be insane—their savagery can be deliberate and intentional, unleashed in carefully directed and rationed bursts. Serial killers, demon cultists, arsonists, dangerous hedonists, and others lured to atrocity by passion are drawn to this alignment.

PHILOSOPHIES

Some chaotic evil characters have coherent philosophies or ideas that guide their actions. However, many—if not most—are driven from within by strong, usually poisonous and unpredictable emotions. Below are some of the more common chaotic evil personality types.

Devotees

Just as some people find solace in upholding order and justice, some swear allegiance to their opposites—the chaos and entropy that eventually grind everything to dust. Whether these devotees are antipaladins, cultists of demon lords, or those who simply feel that the world deserves to be burned down, devotees seek to foster chaos and evil not just for personal gain, but for chaos and evil's own sake. Some believe that the world must be destroyed in order to be rebuilt into something better, or see themselves as a necessary part of an eternal struggle—for light requires darkness to give it contrast. More often, they devote themselves out of a desire to gain power from an evil and chaotic entity, or to impose revenge on a world they feel has wronged them.

If you are a devotee, you:

- Deliberately sow chaos and pain for their own sakes, rather than to obtain personal reward.
- May worship a demon lord or another personification of chaos and evil.
- Find spiritual satisfaction in destruction.

Code: Chaos is the true nature of existence, and it will eventually reclaim its own, so you help it along.

Furies

Furies are driven by a rage so consuming that it can never be satisfied. For some, this rage is birthed from a truly horrific past—perhaps one in which they suffered at the hands of another fury. In other cases, it is caused by disgust or despair ignited after witnessing too much depravity. In still others, the cause is simply a sense of stymied entitlement, or even a natural disposition untempered by reason. Not all furies are immediately identifiable as such—some bank their anger, burning slow but hot, and can conceal their temperaments and their actions, corrupting and undermining rather than rampaging. They may find justifications for their rage in the failings (real or imagined) of others, or they may not feel a need to justify themselves at all. Regardless of their motives, a festering, white-hot fever of rage is at the heart of all they do.

If you are a fury, you:

- Are prone to outbursts of violence—whether physical, verbal, or psychological.
- Often redirect anger toward convenient targets, punishing innocents for minor offenses.
- Feel empowered and invigorated when unleashing your anger, and may see patience and calm as weaknesses.
  Code: If you hurt them, they must have deserved it.

Hedonists

To evil hedonists, nothing matters except personal pleasure, and it's only natural and right to grab as much of it as they can. Any consequences are secondary, if they are considered at all. Classic evil hedonists live in the moment and take what they want by force. These are the people who burn down a city because their hands are cold, or kill a family just to steal their horse. While other personality types may have a greater sense of entitlement, hedonists are characterized by their unwillingness to restrict themselves unnecessarily—and to a hedonist, all restrictions seem unnecessary.

If you are a hedonist, you:

- Follow your whims and passions, regardless of the potential consequences.
- May get bored easily and seek out ever-greater taboos to break.
- Have disproportionate responses to irritation.
  Code: Because you felt like it, that's why.

ADVANTAGES AND CHALLENGES

Whether because they act on every whim, or because they take monstrous shortcuts in pursuit of their goals, chaotic evil characters can be hard to upper hand, making it difficult for rivals and enemies to gain the initiative against them. Their vicious passions may or may not be worn on their sleeves, but even when they're working in arrangements that are generally favorable to them, few chaotic evil characters can tolerate structure or self-control for long periods without lashing out or breaking the rules. Those who rule over chaotic evil creatures must usually do so with an iron fist, as many such creatures can be controlled only with violence and threats.

For all that, lack of reflection and an overreliance on emotions when making decisions can make some chaotic evil characters easy to manipulate for those (usually evil) characters who can get inside their heads. When properly harnessed, their savage destruction can be extremely useful, a tidal wave unleashed on command by their masters.

OPPORTUNITIES AND ALLIES

Antipaladins, as unholy counterparts to paladins, must be chaotic evil. Barbarians (whose strength is fueled by wrath) are good choices for classic out-of-control, animalistic butchers; inquisitors with the destruction judgment or magi could work well, too. Bards and oracles are well

placed to play more insidious, corrupting, or maddening roles, whether as royal advisors or demagogues.

Potential chaotic evil allies on Golarion include the following forces.

Chaotic Evil Regions: Belkzen's savage orcs are strongly chaotic evil, as are the gnoll bands of Garund's Brazen Peaks. Evil leaking out from Rovagug's cage has long since made the Darklands a place of cruelty and terror, as evidenced by nations of evil fey, drow, serpentfolk, and ghouls. In Tian Xia, the kraken Zhanagorr's brutal rule stamps its alignment on the coastal nation of Wanshou.

Demon Cults: The Worldwound and Kyonin's Tanglebriar are obvious incursions of chaotic evil into reality, but demons conduct their vile work all over Golarion. Whether you worship a demon lord or simply find demons to be like-minded purveyors of destruction, the Abyss's residents have much to offer the agents of chaos.

Monstrous Races: Many monstrous races, particularly those who worship Lamashtu or Rovagug, are embodiments of chaotic evil in its most savage and unthinking form. From malicious orcs to the Spawn of Rovagug, chaotic evil creatures threaten the borders of every civilized nation.

TRAITS

The following traits suit a chaotic evil alignment:

Bloody-Minded (Combat): You are always ready for bloodshed. You gain a +1 trait bonus on initiative and Intimidate checks.

Passionate Inertia (Social): Your passions drive your thinking so irresistibly that even magic struggles to change your mind. You gain a +2 trait bonus on Will saves to resist having your mind changed about something, but you take a –1 penalty on Will saves to resist temptation and compulsions you might reasonably be already inclined toward.

DENS OF EVIL

While evil can originate anywhere—even in goodly lands such as revolutionary Andoran and war-torn Nirmathas, where the edicts of righteousness and virtue are fervently espoused—vileness breeds more readily in locales where the leadership or ruling structure is corrupt. In lands such as Cheliax and Nidal, evil is the law, not the exception, and characters who hail from these nations are more likely to be of a wicked bent than those from just about anywhere else, resulting from years of either being desensitized to cruelty or free to indulge any wicked whims that strike their fancy.

Evil Nations

While shadowy assassins' guilds and insane cultists are found in dark corners throughout the Inner Sea region, some countries are so infused with primal vileness or are inhabited by so many evil miscreants that their entire governing doctrine is seeded in wretchedness.

Complementing the nation-specific regional traits listed below, the following social trait is useful to evil characters who wish to spread their corrupt agenda throughout other lands.

Wicked Leader (Social): You gain a +1 trait bonus on Charisma checks against evil creatures. If you select the Leadership feat or the Vile Leadership feat (see page 14) at any point when you meet the prerequisites for that feat, you can recruit a cohort who is up to 1 level lower than you (instead of the normal requirement that your cohort must be 2 or more levels lower than you) as long as your cohort is evil.

Cheliax

Few Chelaxians realize their empire's lost potential—how thoroughly the fiendish courts of House Thrune and its many rivals could still rule over the disparate regions of Avistan or perhaps even the entire Inner Sea region. Perhaps you seek to reclaim the empire's faded glory, or maybe you seek to make a name for yourself as part of one of Cheliax's ruling houses. If you hail from Cheliax, you could be a Hellknight spreading the iron fist of law, an infernal binder training at the Egorian Academy of Magical Arts, or a cunning noble house emissary advancing your family's agenda throughout the nation.

Social Slaver (Cheliax): Your upbringing has accustomed you to commanding those you deem inferior. You gain a +2 trait bonus on Intimidate checks against creatures one or more size categories smaller than yourself. The DC of compulsion spells cast by you against smaller creatures increases by 1.

Geb

Geb is infamous for its undead ruling class, but living residents have their place in the Domain of the Dead as well. Individuals born and raised in Geb often view undeath as the logical successor to life, and they strive to earn their own stations in the unliving hierarchy of the nation. If you hail from Geb, you may be an aspiring Blood Lord learning at the Ebon Mausoleum, a vindictive escaped slave hoping to exact revenge on your abusive undead masters, or even a half-living warrior or wizard born of the union of an undead and a mortal (a dhampir, for example; see page 89 of *Pathfinder RPG Bestiary 2* or pages 18–21 of *Pathfinder Player Companion: Blood of the Night*).

Obsequious Morsel (Geb): Survival in Geb requires convincing your betters that you would be of more service to them if they let you live another day than if they turn you into an unliving thrall, and you have mastered the art of buying time against undead attacks. Once per day as a swift action, you can use *sanctuary* as a spell-like ability (caster level = your highest caster level, or 1st if you have no caster level), with a DC equal to 10 + 1/2 your caster level (minimum 0) + your Charisma modifier. Only undead must save to attack you (other creature types are not affected). The effect ends as soon as you attack a creature, as normal.

Nidal

The region now known as Nidal sold itself to Zon-Kuthon in antiquity, but its people continue to live in that god's shadow to this day. Most Nidalese live in constant fear of the benighted nation's aristocratic governing body, the Umbral Court, but there are plenty who seek to curry favor from the nation's lords or take advantage of the terror they inspire. If you hail from Nidal, you may be a proselytizing cleric of the Midnight Lord, a summoner of dark beings from the Shadow Plane, or an unscrupulous charlatan capitalizing on the everyday fears of common people of Nidal.

Shadowsight (Nidal): Your people's ancient compact with Zon-Kuthon manifests strongly in you. While the darkness remains fearsome, you can at least see what lurks there. As a swift action once per day, your eyes can pierce the surrounding darkness—you gain the benefit of low-light vision for a number of rounds equal to your level.

Razmiran

The so-called Theocracy of the Living God, Razmiran is home to many evils, not the least of which are the ruthless clergy who spread word of their ruler and deity. Wearing ominous masks made of iron and wielding terrible maces, these priests proselytize to the masses both within their borders and beyond, rewarding those who listen with much-needed medicines or healing while brutally punishing those who reject Razmir's ways. If you hail from Razmiran, you may be a brusque soldier enforcing the Living God's will, a traveling cleric spreading the word of your beloved deity, or a scornful rebel seeking to set yourself up as a rival deity.

Divine Deceiver (Razmiran): You are trained in the methods of Razmir's priesthood, and can use your arcana to fuel minor healing powers. Once per day as a full-round action, you can sacrifice a prepared arcane spell or spell slot to manifest healing magic. This acts as *cure light wounds*, except you heal 1d6 points of damage per level of the spell or spell slot sacrificed (maximum 5d6) and the hit points healed are temporary (lasting 1 hour).

The Worldwound

The source of an unprecedented invasion of the Material Plane by the demonic forces of the Abyss, the Worldwound is possibly the single greatest source of evil on Golarion today. The spawn of fiends and humans, tieflings (see *Pathfinder Player Companion: Blood of Fiends* and *Pathfinder RPG Bestiary* 264) often hail from this damned region, and some of them are trained either to serve their demonic forebears or to fight against them. The unholy blood coursing through their veins urges them to perform atrocities not of this world. If you hail from the Worldwound, you may be a Sarkorian refugee seeking revenge for your lost tribal lands, an agent of the demonic hordes issuing forth from the Worldwound, or a low templar fighting against the demonic incursion for your own selfish reasons.

Wardbreaker (The Worldwound): You have studied techniques designed to pierce magical protections, with the goal of assisting your Abyssal masters in bringing down the *wardstones* that guard the borders of Mendev. Once per day, you can attempt a melee touch attack against an opponent that you believe has a deflection bonus to AC. If your attack

EVIL PLANES

There is plenty of wicked work to be done on the Material Plane, but why stop there? In addition to many extraplanar bastions ripe for pillaging and depravity, the Great Beyond is also home to some of the most despicable creatures in the multiverse. For those bold enough to brave the wicked aspects of the Inner Sphere or venture into the damnable Outer Planes, there is much to be gained by venturing into Hell, Abaddon, the Abyss, or any of the other countless demiplanes that boast evil masters.

The Inner Sphere is home to two prominent evil planes: the Plane of Shadow (also known as the Shadow Plane) and the Plane of Negative Energy (also known as the Negative Energy Plane). While the Shadow Plane is a sort of dark mirror of the Material Plane—and thus boasts familiar-yet-sinister locations such as Shadow Absalom and Shadow Sothis—this is not true of the Negative Energy Plane. Instead, the Negative Energy Plane is the birthplace of abominable unlife, including many of the undead that stalk Golarion.

The Outer Sphere is riddled with evil planes, including one of the vilest realms of all, the Abyss. Elsewhere in the sphere, the nine layers of Hell form a baleful nesting box of evil realms, while the dark mists of Abaddon serve as a wasteland for the life-hating, soul-stealing daemons and their ilk. Travelers should tread cautiously in all these planes, but for those willing to risk their lives (and their souls) there, much evil power lies waiting to be gained.

is successful, your foe's deflection bonus to AC is halved (to a minimum of +0) for a number of rounds equal to your Charisma modifier. You can use this ability twice per day at 10th level and three times per day at 20th level.

OTHER DENS OF EVIL

Many other lands likewise cast shadows on their people's hearts and souls. The witches of Irrisen have long sought to spread their eternal winter. The pirates of the Shackles come in all flavors, including both bloodthirsty buccaneers and amoral charming rogues. In the Mwangi Expanse, pockets of corruption fester; the mummified god-king of Mzali inspires his people to hate all outsiders, while the denizens of Usaro are ruthless demon worshipers. While the people of the Sodden Lands might be pitied, many—particularly the cannibalistic Koboto—adjusted to their circumstances in horrifying ways. Far to the north, the people of Kalva likewise practice cannibalism within the Linnorm Kingdom of Icemark.

Even bastions of goodness can produce misfits—an Andoren abolitionist might commit atrocities for his cause, burning plantations to the ground and murdering entire slave-owning families. Hermean exiles may be so convinced of their superior breeding that they seek a kingdom to call their own. The potential for evil exists within everyone, and any corner of Golarion might be the breeding ground for the next Whispering Tyrant.

ORGANIZED EVIL

Meddlesome bands of heroes often try to take power from those who have already rightfully seized it for themselves. While the wicked have an inclination toward self-interest, wise individuals know there is strength in numbers even among the corrupt. Evil adventurers seeking like-minded allies could do worse than to consider the Vile Leadership feat or join one of the following ambitious evil organizations.

VILE LEADERSHIP

You rule over your own cabal of minions with a villainous cohort as your lieutenant.

Prerequisites: Character level 7th, good standing with an evil organization (see page 15 for examples).

Benefits: You can attract a loyal cohort and a number of cowed followers to assist you in your journeys. This feat is similar to Leadership, except Vile Leadership rewards—rather than hinders—leaders who have cruel reputations or who cause the deaths of their followers. Once you take this feat, you cannot take the Leadership feat without retraining your feat selection (see *Pathfinder RPG Ultimate Campaign* 191 for the rules on retraining feats).

In order to benefit from this feat, you must belong to one of the evil organizations listed in this section and also be in good standing with that organization. This is most easily accomplished by performing a weekly or monthly tribute for the organization. Each organization requires a different kind of tribute; see Evil Organizations on page 15 for example groups and their appropriate tributes.

Numerous factors can affect your Vile Leadership score (which acts as a Leadership score for the purpose of feats and abilities that rely on a Leadership score, other than Leadership itself); work with your GM and use the tables below to adjust your Vile Leadership score. The NPCs you attract must be affiliated with the evil organization to which you belong.

Vile Leadership Modifiers

A leader's reputation affects here Vile Leadership score.

Leader's Reputation	Modifier
Ruthless	+2
Rewards loyalty/success	+1
Possesses a special power	+1
Indecisive	−1
Tolerant of failure	−1
Merciful	−2

Other modifiers may apply when you try to attract a cohort with this feat, as listed below.

Leader's Attributes	Modifier
Gained power by eliminating a superior	+1
Fails to punish or kill minions who make costly mistakes	−2*
Recruits a cohort of a different alignment	−1

* Cumulative per incident of compassion shown. This penalty is incurred even if you show mercy to avoid killing or punishing more than 20% of your minions during a given character level (see the footnote to the following table on page 15).

Followers have different priorities from cohorts. When you try to attract a follower with this feat, use the following modifiers.

Leader's Attributes	Modifier
Has a stronghold, base of operations, guildhouse, etc.	+2

Has punished or killed minions to set an example or assert dominance	+1*
Has a tendency toward long periods of inactivity	–1
Restricts minions from looting, pillaging, or pursuing other spoils of war	–1

* Cumulative to a maximum bonus of +1 per character level, with minimum of one minion per incident. If you punish or kill more than 20% of your minions during a given character level, this bonus becomes a penalty instead. At the beginning of a new level, any bonus of penalty from punishing or killing minions resets to 0.

EVIL ORGANIZATIONS

Each of the following organizations includes an example tribute for characters who take the Vile Leadership feat (see the sidebar for additional suitable organizations).

Aspis Consortium

Few villainous organizations rival the size and the scope of the Aspis Consortium, a multinational corporation whose liquid assets alone exceed tens of millions of gold pieces. The Consortium's vast resources are acquired not merely through adroit business practices, but also through devious and ruthless exploitation of the people with whom it trades. The most ambitious members of the Aspis Consortium are said to be so greedy that they would create artificial plagues just so the organization could sell the cure to settlements in need. The Consortium employs a vast army of freelance merchants and swindlers as well as professional soldiers, mercenaries, and unscrupulous thugs, all of whom the company uses to manipulate public perception and obfuscate any appearance of impropriety.

Tribute: Each week, either through roleplaying or the use of skills such as Appraise, Bluff, or Intimidate, you must knowingly swindle or exploit a business partner (likely a stranger such as a merchant or trader) to obtain a profit in gold. Recovery or forceful acquisition of a rare magic item, relic, or piece of lore worth at least 2,000 gp satisfies this requirement for 1 month.

Rushlight Society

Villainous organizations need not always be international powerhouses. The Rushlight Society is a well-organized and well-managed group of bandits dedicated to monetary gain and instilling fear in Varisia's local country folk. The group prides itself on thwarting commerce in and out of Magnimar, except for trade by sea, which it leaves unscathed for reasons known only to the group's leader. In addition to employing ordinary thugs and cons, the bandits sometimes induct wizards and magi into their ranks, using such magicians to charm caravan guards or town militia before ransacking the bewitched defenders' helpless charges.

Tribute: At least once per week, a member of the Rushlight Society must waylay a traveling caravan, participate in a raid or assault on a small town or larger settlement, or commit some other form of commercially influenced mayhem.

OTHER EVIL ORGANIZATIONS

The organizations listed in this section are far from the only villainous groups in the Inner Sea region, let alone on Golarion as a whole. Numerous other cabals, guilds, and dark forces plot and perpetrate tyranny and crime against the innocent, the unaware, and the vulnerable. Players and GMs are encouraged to work together to come up with their own organizations if they so choose. GMs can also come up with fitting tributes for evil groups mentioned in other Pathfinder Player Companions or detailed in other Pathfinder products such as Pathfinder Campaign Setting books and Pathfinder Adventure Paths.

Some groups act with impunity, sanctioned by their government or a ranking leader, and thus are devoid of the secrecy that permeates other groups of organized evil. The Cold Sisters of Whitethrone in Irrisen are feared across the wintry land for their fierce pursuit of both commoners and adventurers who to fail to pay the proper respect (and levies) to the ruling witches of Whitethrone. In Numeria, the Black Sovereign ostensibly rules over the cabal of arcanists known as the Technic League, which in turn oppresses the common Kellids of the surrounding region with harsh taxes and its nigh-invincible technology.

Other groups are less institutionalized and are not known to follow any one leader. The Blackfire Adepts—a mysterious group of spellcasters who infiltrate other arcane circles to facilitate their sinister research and worse—supposedly seek to unravel the very fabric of the multiverse. In the Mana Wastes, while Alkenstar is famous for its feats of engineering, the roving bands of craven mutants and twisted abominations that wander the hinterlands rival the nation's explosive reputation.

Umbral Court

Villainy reigns supreme in the shadow-steeped nation of Nidal (see page 12). No mere organization, the Umbral Court is the ruling body of aristocrats who govern that country. It draws its roots from the warrior clans of ancient times, who pledged their own souls to Zon-Kuthon in the earliest days of the Age of Darkness—and the souls of their descendants for all of time. Members of the Umbral Court are also responsible for the imposition of Nidal's severe laws and the exaltation of pain and suffering. The Court maintains its ancient bargain with the Dark Prince fearlessly and with utmost reverence, and those who prove their loyalty as agents to the Umbral Court can be assured they will be well compensated.

Tribute: A servant of the Umbral Court must perform an act of self-flagellation or self-mortification at the start of each day, dealing at least 1 point of damage to herself per 2 character levels and letting the damage heal naturally (not magically) over the course of the week. Alternatively, a character can remain in good standing with the Umbral Court as long as she acquires and wears a new *Nidalese shadow piercing* (see page 28) at least once per month; this piercing can replace an old one or be in addition to existing piercings.

DEALS WITH DARK POWERS

Many unscrupulous characters willingly go to any lengths to achieve their villainous goals. Such ruthlessness often impacts those unfortunates in their paths, but occasionally evil characters prove to be the greatest victims of their own ambitions. Among the planes, foul forces eye the mortal realm intently, eager to corrupt and ready to feed. When called upon, such denizens of the dark readily offer all manner of depraved power. All they wish in return is one's immortal soul.

DAMNATION FEATS

Damnation feats represent a bargain the character has made with some dark power, granting the character great power at the cost of her eternal soul. Damnation feats are distinct from more common feats in three ways.

Damned: A character with a damnation feat is damned (see the sidebar). This is likely a permanent condition, but might be avoided through redemption.

Greater Power: Damnation feats increase in power relative to the number of damnation feats a character possesses. Each new damnation feat increases the power of all of the character's damnation feats, including the newly taken feat and future feats.

Patronage: All damnation feats require the patronage of an evil outsider—typically a daemon, devil, demon, or kyton. This evil outsider patron must be favorably disposed toward the character and must have a number of Hit Dice equal to or greater than her character level. An evil outsider summoned via a spell like planar binding might be coerced to serve as a character's patron (whether that character is the spell's caster or another seeking patronage). The caster of a planar binding spell must still attempt Charisma checks to coerce the outsider into service, but she gains a +4 bonus on her Charisma checks if that service is to act as a damnation feat's patron. Other outsiders might more willingly serve as patrons at the GM's discretion.

Fiendskin (Damnation)

The forces of darkness gird you against the light.

Benefit: You gain defensive abilities related to your patron's outsider subtype. For example, if your patron is a devil, the abilities listed below tie into the devil subtype (see Creature Subtypes, starting on page 310 of the *Pathfinder RPG Bestiary*). These benefits tie to your patron's subtype, not your specific patron (its abilities might differ from the norm).

One Damnation Feat: Choose one of the energy types to which your patron's outsider subtype grants resistance. You gain resistance 5 against that energy type.

Two Damnation Feats: Choose one of the energy types to which your patron's outsider subtype grants resistance. You gain resistance 5 against that energy type. If you already have resistance to the chosen energy type (even from earlier benefits of this feat), this new resistance stacks with the existing resistance.

Three Damnation Feats: Choose one of the energy types to which your patron's outsider subtype grants resistance. You gain immunity to the selected energy type.

Four Damnation Feats: Your creature type changes to outsider (native). Additionally, choose one energy type to which your patron's outsider subtype grants immunity or resistance. You gain immunity to that energy type.

Maleficium (Damnation)

You are a master of dark magic.

Benefit: You cast spells with the evil descriptor with increased potency.

One Damnation Feat: Add 1 to the DCs of all saving throws against spells with the evil descriptor that you cast.

Two Damnation Feats: When you apply a metamagic feat to a spell with the evil descriptor, that spell takes up a spell slot 1 level lower than normal (to a minimum of 1 level above the spell's actual level).

Three Damnation Feats: Add 1 to the DCs of all saving throws against spells with the evil descriptor that you cast. This bonus stacks with the earlier benefits of this feat.

Four Damnation Feats: Treat your caster level as being 2 higher for all level-dependent effects of spells with the evil descriptor that you cast.

Mask of Virtue (Damnation)

Your alignment is known to you and you alone.

Benefit: Those who try to learn your true alignment find it hidden or receive a false result. Depending on the number of damnation feats you possess, spells or special abilities that would normally reveal your alignment return a vague or incorrect result. If this feat disguises your alignment, you can use either your true alignment or the false one when using magic items with alignment prerequisites.

One Damnation Feat: The spell or special ability returns an inconclusive result.

Two Damnation Feats: Upon gaining this power, choose an alignment within one step of your actual alignment. Your alignment is always revealed as being that false alignment.

Three Damnation Feats: Upon gaining this power, choose an alignment within two steps of your actual alignment. Your alignment is always revealed as being this false alignment.

Four Damnation Feats: You immediately know when someone is attempting to use a spell or special ability to learn your alignment. You learn the name and alignment of the creature using the effect. Additionally, you can choose any alignment as the result returned by the spell or ability.

Soulless Gaze (Damnation)

Otherworldly dread infuses your gaze.

Benefit: You can use the Intimidate skill to manipulate and terrify others.

One Damnation Feat: You gain a +2 bonus on Intimidate checks.

Two Damnation Feats: When you demoralize a creatures more than once using Intimidate, you can create stronger fear conditions rather than increasing the duration of the shaken condition.

Three Damnation Feats: You gain a +2 bonus on Intimidate checks (this stacks with the earlier benefits of this feat).

DAMNATION

When a character takes a damnation feat, his soul is damned. The character's spirit is promised to a dark power, whether an evil deity or a foul planar race, and his soul will ultimately be consigned to some grim fate after his death. The method by which one becomes damned typically determines the specifics of this eternal doom, but the in-game effects are the same regardless.

Upon taking a damnation feat, the character's soul becomes ensnared by dark, otherworldly forces. From that point on, if the character dies, returning him to life proves to be more difficult. Any nonevil spellcaster who attempts to bring the character back from the dead must attempt a caster level check (DC = 10 + the slain character's Hit Dice). Success means the spell functions as normal, while failure means the spell fails and cannot be attempted again for 24 hours. Evil spellcasters, however, can raise the slain character normally, without a check.

Upon taking a second damnation feat, the character becomes even more ensnared by his doom. He remains difficult to return from the dead (as noted above), and he can't be affected by *breath of life* or *raise dead*, even when these spells are cast by an evil spellcaster. Also, the character's alignment shifts one step toward evil (typically toward the alignment of whatever creature serves as his patron).

This corruption continues if the character takes a third damnation feat. He is affected as previously noted, and in addition, the spell resurrection no longer affects him. The character's alignment again shifts one step toward evil (typically toward the alignment of whatever creature serves as his patron).

Finally, upon taking a fourth damnation feat, the character can no longer be returned from the dead by any method short of a *wish* or *miracle*. The character's alignment shifts one more step toward the alignment of whatever creature serves as his patron.

Four Damnation Feats: You can use Intimidate to demoralize opponents as a swift action.

Redemption

As long as a character possesses a damnation feat, she experiences the effects of damnation. Only nonevil creatures can retrain damnation feats—they likely do so using the retraining rules presented on page 191 of *Pathfinder RPG Ultimate Campaign*. During this retraining, the character must follow all the usual rules associated with replacing a feat and must be the target of an *atonement* spell cast by a good character. Evil characters seeking to redeem themselves might also make use of the redemption rules on page 18 of *Pathfinder Player Companion: Champions of Purity*. Even after a character has redeemed herself and replaced her damnation feats, whoever had once ensnared her is unlikely to give up on its attempts to corrupt her.

DIVINE INFLUENCE

The gods of darkness and evil wield great power. These malign forces offer a portion of their unholy might to mortals in return for the mortals' unwavering devotion. This section discusses many of these deities, as well as new subdomains available to their followers.

EVIL DEITIES

See the table on the inside front cover for more information about the following gods.

Asmodeus: The Prince of Darkness rewards strength, cunning, and discipline. Warriors, bureaucrats, merchants, and others impose law and order in his name. They profit from guile and crush the weak, while opposing anarchists and so-called "freedom fighters."

Dahak: Dahak's non-dragon worshipers are often dragonslayers, especially those who hunt metallic dragons. Others serve dragons or creatures like serpentfolk, spreading destruction and chaos in the name of their scaled masters.

Fumeiyoshi: Fumeiyoshi's humanoid followers are unrepentant fallen paladins and rogue samurai, for the most part. Those who venerate him as the god of graves work alongside putrid undead creatures to terrorize and punish the living.

General Susumu: Worshipers of the Black Daimyo revel in the glory of battle and believe in the rightness of physical strength and conquest. The most ruthless of his followers start devastating conflicts just to engage in bloody combat.

Gyronna: The women of Gyronna's faith are infiltrators and corruptors. They twist the minds of people against one another, filling them with rage and hatred that destroys the communities where their evil spreads.

Lady Nanbyo: The Widow of Suffering commands those who serve her to heap sorrow upon sorrow through acts such as intentionally spreading terrible diseases among the victims of a recent flood, fire, or earthquake.

Lamashtu: Followers of the Mother of Monsters spread fear, madness, and corruption in the name of their demon goddess. They sometimes secretly raise vile creatures and then unleash these beasts upon innocent victims.

Lao Shu Po: Old Rat Woman's agents are thieves and scoundrels who perform foul deeds under the cover of darkness. Like the goddess they serve, they steal power and wealth through subterfuge.

Norgorber: Norgorber's worshipers vary, depending on which aspect of the deity they venerate. They might be members of murder cults, skilled assassins, hidden spies, or seemingly omniscient rumormongers.

Rovagug: Those who serve the Rough Beast seek the destruction of all. They may develop complicated plans, but the savagery with which they execute such plans makes it appear as if they were fueled by nothing but mindless rage.

Urgathoa: The Pallid Princess has many living followers. They spread disease and encourage excessive indulgences in exchange for promises of physical pleasure and the power of undeath.

Yaezhing: Yaezhing's most active followers are vigilantes who retaliate against real and perceived transgressions, often exacting punishments that far outweigh the crimes committed. Others are cold-hearted murderers.

Zon-Kuthon: Zon-Kuthon's followers are twisted souls who exalt pain and suffering as enlightenment. They spread misery to prepare the world for their god's rise to dominion over all.

SUBDOMAINS

Presented here are new subdomains that, at your GM's discretion, can be substituted for one of a deity's granted domains. Suggested deities that may optionally grant the use of the following subdomains are listed in the entry for each subdomain.

Cannibalism Subdomain

Associated Domain: Evil.

    Associated Deities: Lamashtu, Rovagug, Urgathoa.

    Replacement Power: The following granted power replaces the touch of evil ability of the Evil domain.

    Consume the Enemy (Su): As a full-round action that is considered an evil act and provokes attacks of opportunity, you can bite a helpless living or freshly killed creature, dealing 1d3 points of damage. By consuming the creature's flesh, you gain a +1 profane bonus on saving throw DCs for all spells, spell-like abilities, and supernatural abilities you use against creatures of the same type (and subtype, if humanoid or outsider) as the cannibalized creature. This effect lasts for a number of minutes equal to 1/2 your cleric level or until you use this ability against a different creature. At 5th, 10th, 15th, and 20th level, this bonus increases by 1 (+5 maximum). You can use this ability a number of times per day equal to 3 + your Wisdom modifier.

    Replacement Domain Spells: 1st—*magic fang*, 2nd—*enemy's heart*^{ARG}, 3rd—*greater magic fang*.

Corruption Subdomain

Associated Domain: Evil.

    Associated Deities: Asmodeus, Dahak, General Susumu, Gyronna, Lamashtu, Rovagug, Urgathoa.

    Replacement Power: The following granted power replaces the scythe of evil ability of the Evil domain.

    Spark Malfeasance (Su): At 8th level, you can awaken the sinful desires of a target within 30 feet with a ranged touch attack. The target suffers extreme guilt and is sickened for a number of rounds equal to 1/2 your cleric level. To end the effect earlier, the target can willingly commit an evil act (if it is of good alignment) or attempt a Will save (DC = 10

+ 1/2 your cleric level + your Wisdom modifier) at the beginning of its turn each round. Creatures that succeed at their saving throws are immune to this ability for 24 hours. You can use this ability once per day at 8th level, and an additional time per day for every 4 levels beyond 8th.

Replacement Domain Spells: 2nd—*suggestion*, 6th—*greater bestow curse*.

Demodand Subdomain

Associated Domains: Chaos, Evil.

Associated Deities: Rovagug, Yaezhing.

Replacement Power: The following granted power replaces the touch of evil ability of the Evil domain or the touch of chaos ability of the Chaos domain.

Faith-Stealing Strike (Su): You can make a single melee attack using your highest base attack bonus against a creature capable of casting divine spells. If you damage the creature, it must succeed at a Will save (DC = 10 + 1/2 your cleric level + your Wisdom modifier) or be unable to cast any divine spells for 1 round. If you do not damage your target with the attack, this ability is expended with no effect. You can use this ability a number of times per day equal to 3 + your Wisdom modifier.

Replacement Domain Spells: 2nd—*align weapon* (chaos or evil only), 6th—*corrosive consumption*^{UM}.

Greed Subdomain

Associated Domain: Trickery.

Associated Deities: Asmodeus, Dahak, Lao Shu Po, Norgorber.

Replacement Power: The following granted power replaces the copycat ability of the Trickery domain.

More for Me (Su): When another character within 30 feet casts a spell with a range greater than touch, you can attempt a caster level check as an immediate action (DC = 15 + the spell's level). If you succeed at the check, you receive the spell's benefit instead of one of the spell's intended targets (chosen by you). If you are already a target of the spell, you are affected as though you were targeted by the same spell twice (which may or may not benefit you; remember that bonuses from the same source do not stack). This ability does not grant you knowledge of the spell being cast. You can use this ability a number of times per day equal to 3 + your Wisdom modifier.

Replacement Domain Spells: 2nd—*masterwork transformation*^{UM}, 6th—*guards and wards*, 8th—*create demiplane*^{UM}.

Hatred Subdomain

Associated Domain: Destruction.

Associated Deities: Dahak, Fumeiyoshi, Gyronna, Lady Nanbyo, Rovagug.

Replacement Power: The following granted power replaces the destructive aura ability of the Destruction domain.

Hateful Aura (Su): At 8th level, you can emit a 30-foot aura of hatred for a number of rounds per day equal to your cleric level. These rounds need not be consecutive. Enemies within this aura must attempt a Will save (DC = 10 + 1/2 your cleric level + your Wisdom modifier). Characters who fail their save are filled with hatred, and cannot consider other characters allies for the purpose of any actions or use any teamwork feats. The effect ends immediately if the creature leaves the aura, you end the aura as a free action, or you expend all rounds of this ability.

Replacement Domain Spells: 1st—*murderous command*^{UM}, 2nd—*wrathful mantle*^{APG}.

Kyton Subdomain

Associated Domains: Evil, Law.

Associated Deities: Zon-Kuthon.

Replacement Power: The following granted power replaces the scythe of evil ability of the Evil domain or the staff of order ability of the Law domain.

Pain Is Power (Su): At 8th level, after taking damage from any source, you may attempt a DC 25 concentration check as an immediate action. If you succeed, you gain the benefits of a *blessing of fervor*^{APG} spell for a number of rounds equal to 1/2 your cleric level. If you fail, this ability is expended with no effect. You can use this ability once at 8th level, plus an additional time for every 4 levels you are beyond 8th.

Replacement Domain Spells: 1st—*delay pain*^{UM}, 2nd—*instrument of agony*^{UC}, 3rd—*agonize*^{UM}, 5th—*symbol of pain*.

CALCULATED VILLAINY

Not all evil is about wanton destruction and fulfilling dark whims. Often, it is committed with meticulous planning. A ruthless warlord seeking to expand his borders or exterminate a rebellion; a cunning vizier manipulating the kingdom from behind the throne; a bloodthirsty serial killer choosing the victim, location, and time of her next kill—all of these villains know the value of preparation. Characters like this might well be highly visible and productive members of society, never exposing their hidden selves until the situation and their elaborate plans call for it.

BETRAYAL FEATS

"Teamwork" is a relative term. Many villains don't concern themselves with collateral damage and make their plans with exceeding ruthlessness. Presented below are several teamwork feats with the common theme of reaping a benefit at your allies' expense. All of these feats refer to an initiator and an abettor. The initiator is the one activating the feat (also referred to as "you") and the abettor is an ally who also has the feat and whose presence and (perhaps unwilling) sacrifice allows the feat to take effect. Choosing one of these feats effectively grants consent for an ally with the same feat to harm you in combat, and vice versa, but evil characters are often willing to take big risks to get the upper hand. Some recruit devoted minions specifically to use in this way. Characters with class abilities granting allies access to teamwork feats (such as cavaliers or inquisitors) can select these teamwork feats normally, but allies who are granted these feats can use the feats only as initiators, not as abettors. An inquisitor could not grant an ally the Ally Shield feat and then use the ally as a shield, for example, but he could allow that ally to use him as a shield.

Ally Shield (Betrayal, Teamwork)

You are willing to use your allies as shields to ward off attacks aimed at you.

Benefit: Whenever you are the target of a melee or ranged attack and are adjacent to an ally who also has this feat, you can initiate this feat to skillfully pull the abettor into harm's way or dodge behind the abettor as an immediate action. You gain cover against that attack (and only that attack). If the attack misses you but would have hit you if not for the cover bonus to your Armor Class, the abettor becomes the target of the attack and the attacker must make a new attack roll (with all the same modifiers) against the abettor's Armor Class.

Callous Casting (Betrayal, Teamwork)

You don't care if your allies are harmed by your spells. The smart ones know this and start running.

Prerequisite: Spellcraft 1 rank.

Benefit: You initiate this feat by including an abetting ally in the area of any spell that deals damage of a type to which the abettor is not immune. The callousness of the attack disheartens foes in the area, who must succeed at a Will save against the spell's DC or be shaken for 1 round per spell level. After you resolve the spell's effects, the abettor can move up to her speed as an immediate action. Any movement undertaken using this action is then subtracted from her speed until the end of her next turn. This movement can still provoke attacks of opportunity as normal. Once a foe has attempted a Will save against this feat, he is immune to this effect from that initiator for 24 hours thereafter.

Friendly Fire (Betrayal, Teamwork)

Your ranged attacks startle your enemies, partly because you're not even trying to avoid hitting your allies.

Prerequisite: Precise Shot.

Benefit: You initiate this feat as a standard action, making a ranged attack against a foe engaged in melee with at least one abettor. This shot deliberately forsakes normal precautions, putting your abettor at risk, but also is unexpected enough to surprise your mutual opponent. You gain a +2 bonus on your attack roll if the attack passes through an abettor's space. If your shot misses the target, you must immediately make a second attack roll with all the same modifiers against the abettor, potentially hitting her with the attack instead of the opponent. When the attack resolves (regardless of whether either potential target was hit), the intended target's startled reaction provokes an attack of opportunity from the abettor.

Reckless Moves (Betrayal, Teamwork)

You and your teammates push and pull each other to maintain your balance in precarious circumstances.

Prerequisite: Acrobatics 3 ranks.

Benefit: If you are adjacent to an ally who also has this feat, you can initiate this feat as a free action to use the ally as a counterweight to improve your balance, which requires you to push or pull her slightly. You gain a +4 bonus on Acrobatics, Climb, and Stealth checks until you cease using this feat as a free action or you move away from the ally. The abettor is kept off balance and takes a −2 penalty on Acrobatics, Climb, and Stealth checks as long as this feat remains in effect. You can initiate this feat as an immediate action while you are falling or being knocked prone in order to switch places with the abettor, moving her into your former space and moving yourself into her former space. If you do, you and the abettor each end this movement prone unless you succeed at an Acrobatics check with a DC of 20 (the bonuses and penalties for this feat apply). If you were falling, the abettor is falling instead. If you or the abettor were climbing, the other person must succeed at a Climb check against the surface's normal DC to grab on and avoid falling. Switching places provokes attacks of opportunity for the abettor only.

Splash Volley (Betrayal, Teamwork)

Your allies are used to being in the splash zone of your hurled weapons, and try to ensure that at least your opponent gets hit.

Prerequisite: Base attack bonus +1.

Benefit: You initiate this feat whenever you throw a splash weapon into a square within the reach of an ally who also has this feat and miss your target. Rather than you rolling to see where the weapon lands, the abettor can try to redirect it as an immediate action by making a melee touch attack against any adjacent foe. If the abettor's attack hits that foe, the splash weapon impacts in the nearest square the targeted foe occupies.

Wild Flanking (Betrayal, Teamwork)

When flanking, you use your position to rain grievous blows upon a trapped foe, though you have little regard to the well-being of your flanking partner as you wildly hack away.

Prerequisites: Power Attack, base attack bonus +4.

Benefit: When you are flanking an opponent with an ally who also possesses this feat, you can throw yourself into your attacks in such a way that your opponent takes extra damage, at the risk of these attacks striking your ally as well. When you choose to use this feat, check the results of your attack roll against both your opponent's AC and your ally's AC. If you hit your opponent, you deal bonus damage as though you were using Power Attack. If you hit your ally, the ally takes no damage from your attack except this bonus damage. It is possible to hit both your enemy and your abettor with one attack. Extra damage from this feat stacks with Power Attack.

NEW ROOMS

What is a villain without a lair? Below are additional room options for evil characters using the downtime rules in Chapter 2 of *Pathfinder RPG Ultimate Campaign*.

BLOOD SPA

Benefit temporary age penalty reduction
Create 10 Goods, 4 Influence, 7 Labor, 6 Magic (1,060 gp); **Time** 28 days
Size 4–8 squares
Upgrades From Bath

This room houses a sumptuous tub and alchemical piping that allow a villain to alleviate some of the effects of aging by bathing in the blood of a freshly killed humanoid of less than middle age. The corpse is suspended over the tub via ceiling clamps that can be recessed out of sight in the ceiling. Bathing for an hour in this room reduces any ability score penalties from advanced age by 1 for a duration of 1 week and makes the bather appear younger. Multiple treatments stack. Each corpse provides enough blood for only 1 treatment.

EXECUTION YARD

Earnings Influence +10
Benefit bonus on Intimidate checks
Create 8 Goods, 2 Influence, 10 Labor (420 gp); **Time** 24 days
Size 20–40 squares
Upgrades From Courtyard

This open area is used to host public executions. The execution device, such as a headsman's block or gallows, occupies a dais in the yard's center. Surrounding it are viewing galleries for guests of assorted status and plenty of standing room for lower-class rabble. Gibbets or pikes around the yard display the condemned, granting a +3 bonus on Intimidate checks within the settlement to whoever publicly ordered the execution.

Destructive Tendencies

One of evil's strongest lures is that it allows you to do whatever you want, whenever you want to do it, regardless of society's mores. However, only those with the power to take what they want without repercussion and defeat those who dare oppose them can truly indulge their darkest desires. For many, that power comes from having a sharp blade and a strong arm to wield it.

If you want something, one of the simplest and most direct ways to get it is to taking it from someone else. If you are bigger, faster, or have better weapons, why waste time and energy earning wages to buy things or developing skills to craft them? You may not even need to fight anyone if your threat of force is convincing enough. Sometimes, all you have to do is break things—things that are important to people or things that make lots of noise—to show that you could do more serious damage if you so choose. Let the wizards and the clerics cast their flashy spells, if they must. When a warrior speaks with violence, the message is always clear.

Dread Vanguard (Antipaladin Archetype)

Some antipaladins serve or ally themselves with villains who are bent on earthly conquest. They care nothing for the intricacies of divine spellcasting, but malevolent energy still surrounds them. Whether alone or at the head of a marauding host, these cruel warriors bring suffering and death—but their presence also heralds the coming of a greater evil.

Dread vanguards have the following class features.

Beacon of Evil (Su): A dread vanguard unleashes the powers of his vile masters to strengthen both himself and his allies.

At 4th level and every 4 level thereafter, a dread vanguard gains one additional use of his touch of corruption ability per day. As a standard action, he can spend a use of his touch of corruption ability to manifest the darkness in his soul as an area of flickering shadows with a 30-foot radius centered on him. These shadows don't affect visibility. The antipaladin and all allies in the area gain a +1 morale bonus to AC and on attack rolls, damage rolls, and saving throws against fear, and also ignore the first 5 points of hardness when attacking unattended inanimate objects. This lasts for 1 minute, as long as the dread vanguard is conscious.

At 8th level, the aura grants fast healing 3 to the dread vanguard as well as to his allies while they remain within it. Additionally, while this aura is active, the antipaladin can use his touch of corruption ability against any targets within its radius by making a ranged touch attack.

At 12th level, when he activates this ability, a dread vanguard can choose to increase the radius of one antipaladin aura he possesses to 30 feet. Also, the morale

bonus granted to AC and on attack rolls, damage rolls, and saving throws against fear increases to +2.

At 16th level, the fast healing granted by this ability increases to 5. Additionally, the antipaladin's weapons and those of his allies within the aura's radius are considered evil for the purpose of overcoming damage reduction.

At 20th level, the beacon of evil's radius increases to 60 feet, and the morale bonus granted to AC and on attack rolls, damage rolls, and saving throws against fear increases to +4. Lastly, attacks made by the dread vanguard and his allies within the aura's radius are infused with pure unholy power, and deal an additional 1d6 points of damage.

This ability replaces the spells class feature. A dread vanguard does not gain any spells or spellcasting abilities, cannot use spell trigger or spell completion magic items, and does not have a caster level from this class.

Dark Emissary (Sp): At 14th level, a dread vanguard becomes a true messenger of the forces of darkness he serves. Once per day, the dread vanguard can expend two uses of his touch of corruption ability to mark one location within 60 feet with the stain of evil. This location can be any point in space, but the ability works best if placed on an altar, shrine, or other site important to a community. The location is affected as if by a *desecrate* spell. Creatures approaching within 30 feet of the site must succeed at a Will save or suffer the effects of *crushing despair*.

At 17th level, the dread vanguard can also mark the site with a *symbol of pain*, and at 20th level, he adds a *symbol of weakness*. If available, all three of these effects overlap. Creatures must save against each effect individually, and the effects stack. The caster level for all effects is equal to the dread vanguard's class level. The save DC is equal to 10 + 1/2 the antipaladin's level + his Charisma modifier. A location remains marked in this way for up to 1 day per antipaladin level. During this time, the *crushing despair* and *symbols* are triggered when the first target enters each spell's area. They remain active for 10 minutes, then can be triggered again if targets are within range. If the effects are disabled, they become inactive for 10 minutes, but then can be triggered again as normal. *Dispel magic* and similar spells suppress the effects, and all effects of dark emissary can be removed by a *consecrate* spell cast on the location by a cleric of a level equal to or higher than the dread vanguard.

Allies or evil creatures who serve the same power or organization as the dread vanguard are immune to the *crushing despair* and *symbol* effects, and automatically know that the location has been marked for their masters. They can treat this location as very familiar for the purpose of *teleport* and similar spells and can use *scrying* and related spells as though they were familiar with any subject within 20 feet of it. At 14th level, a dread vanguard can have one marked site active at a time. At

17th and 20th levels, he can add one additional site that is simultaneously active. Marking a new site beyond this limit ends all effects on the oldest active site. This ability replaces aura of sin.

New Combat Feats

The following feats help make bloodshed and violence more effective tools for achieving one's goals.

Chairbreaker (Combat)

You deal more damage by breaking nearby objects against your enemies.

Prerequisites: Catch Off-Guard, base attack bonus +1.

Benefit: When you attack a target with an improvised weapon, you can give that weapon the broken condition to deal 1d4 points of additional damage on that attack. Additionally, you gain a +4 bonus on the roll to confirm a critical hit with this attack. If you confirm the crit, the extra damage granted by this feat is also multiplied and the improvised weapon is destroyed.

Destructive Persuasion (Combat)

Sometimes, you have to break things if you want people to get your point.

Prerequisites: Str 13, Power Attack, Intimidate 1 rank.

Benefit: As a standard action, you can attempt to smash an unattended inanimate object while attempting an Intimidate check (see Smashing an Object, *Pathfinder RPG Core Rulebook* 173). If you break the object, you gain a bonus to the Intimidate check equal to half its hardness (minimum +1). If you destroy the object, the bonus is equal to its hardness (minimum +1). Creatures intimidated by this feat cannot be affected by it again for 24 hours.

Shrapnel Strike (Combat)

You can bash things to damage nearby opponents.

Prerequisites: Str 15, Improved Sunder, Power Attack.

Benefit: When you attempt a Strength check to break an object that can shatter (nothing made of paper, cloth, leather, or other soft, pliable material), you gain a bonus on the Strength check equal to your base attack bonus. If you surpass the object's break DC, you can send shards of its material flying out in all directions, dealing an amount of piercing, slashing, and bludgeoning damage equal to 1d4 plus 1 point per point of the object's hardness to all creatures within 10 feet of the object, including yourself. A successful Reflex save (DC = 10 + 1/2 your Hit Dice + your Strength modifier) halves the damage.

Stunning Irruption (Combat)

When you smash your way into a room, you gain more than just the element of surprise.

Prerequisites: Str 15, Power Attack, base attack bonus +5.

Benefit: Before starting combat, you can attempt to break through a door, window, or wall to enter a room. If you succeed, the violence of your arrival is so great that all characters within 20 feet of your entry point must succeed at a Fortitude saving throw (DC = 10 + your base attack bonus) or be stunned instead of acting in the surprise round (if there is one) plus 1 round thereafter. Characters who succeed at this save are instead shaken for 1d4 rounds.

HUNGRY FOR POWER

While some villains commit evil deeds in the name of an alien god or to push some inverted morality, for many, evil is simply the by-product of their own selfishness. These ambitious, callous individuals think nothing of sacrificing allies or ripping apart the lives of their rivals or innocent bystanders, if it helps them get ahead. Being power hungry isn't necessarily as obvious as other forms of wickedness—but is often at least as chilling, for such villains exemplify base qualities that lie repressed in even the best of people.

BLOOD SUMMONER (SUMMONER ARCHETYPE)

A blood summoner conjures an eidolon born from violence and blood. These cruel spellcasters are common among the god-callers of now-shattered Sarkoris, where the influence of the Worldwound has warped them into beings of chilling malevolence.

Skills: A blood summoner adds Heal to his list of class skills.

Blood Offering (Su): At 4th level, the blood summoner can sacrifice a flask of blood, extracted up to 1 day ago from a living creature or a corpse that's been dead no longer than 1 minute, to aid and appease an evil outsider within 30 feet as a standard action. This blood can be extracted from a willing or helpless creature as a full-round action that deals 1 point of Constitution damage. The offering grants the outsider a +2 enhancement bonus to the ability score of the blood summoner's choice and grants the blood summoner a +4 circumstance bonus on Diplomacy checks and Charisma checks to bargain with it. The bonuses last for 10 minutes. The offering cannot be made to the same fiend twice in the same day. This ability replaces shield ally.

Blood Travel (Su): At 8th level, a blood summoner can use his maker's call ability to allow his eidolon to travel through the blood of other creatures instead of bringing it to his side. The eidolon can either emerge from the blood of a living creature within range that has fewer than its maximum hit points remaining, or burst from the corpse of a Small or larger creature within range that has been dead for no longer than 1 minute. If the eidolon emerges from an injured creature, that creature takes 4d6 points of damage, which is halved if the creature succeeds at a Fortitude save (DC = 10 + 1/2 the blood summoner's level + his Charisma modifier). The eidolon appears in its choice of the nearest unoccupied square to the creature or corpse it emerged from, and is staggered for 1 round. This ability replaces transposition.

Fiendish Calling (Su): At 10th level, the blood summoner's *summon monster* ability can additionally be used as *lesser planar binding* as a standard action, but only to call evil outsiders. At 13th level, he can instead use it as *planar binding*. At 16th level, he can instead use it as *greater planar binding*. This ability replaces greater shield ally.

Blood Possession (Su): At 16th level as a full-round action, a blood summoner's eidolon can enter and control the body of any corporeal creature that has blood. This ability functions as *marionette possession*[UM], except that the eidolon's body also enters the target and the target can be unwilling. A successful Will save (DC = 10 + 1/2 the blood summoner's level + his Charisma modifier) negates this effect. This ability can be used once per day at 16th level, twice per day at 18th level, and three times per day at 20th level. The eidolon can end this possession at any time as a standard action. If the host body is slain while the eidolon is possessing it, the eidolon is immediately ejected, takes 4d6 points of damage, and is stunned for 1 round. This ability replaces merge forms.

New Summoner Evolutions

The following evolutions appeal to many evil summoners' cruel and disgusting sensibilities.

1-Point Evolutions

The following evolutions cost 1 point from the eidolon's evolution pool.

Bleed (Ex): An eidolon gains the ability to inflict bleeding wounds. Select one type of attack. Attacks of that type deal 1d6 points of bleed damage. This evolution can be selected more than once. Each time an eidolon selects this evolution, it applies to a different attack. The bleed effect doesn't stack.

Slippery (Ex): Due to its slimy hide or a slick exoskeleton, the eidolon is especially slippery. The eidolon gains a +4 bonus to CMD to escape a grapple and on Escape Artist checks.

Sticky (Ex): The eidolon is especially sticky, whether from a coating of adhesive slime, partially congealed blood, or tiny barbed spines. The eidolon gains a +4 bonus on combat maneuver checks to initiate or maintain a grapple.

2-Point Evolution

The following evolution costs 2 points from the eidolon's evolution pool.

Sickening (Ex): The eidolon's smell or appearance is so offensive it sickens nearby creatures. Any living creature except its summoner that approaches within 20 feet or begins its turn in that area is sickened for 1 round unless it succeeds at a Fortitude save (DC = 10 + 1/2 the eidolon's HD + its Con modifier). Creatures that successfully save cannot be affected by the same eidolon's sickening effect for 24 hours.

3-Point Evolution

The following evolution costs 3 points from the eidolon's evolution pool.

Fiendish Appearance (Ex): The eidolon appears as a fiendish creature and manifests some of the abilities of a fiend. Spells and effects that target creatures with the evil subtype or have specific effects against such creatures affect the eidolon as if it had that subtype. The eidolon gains a +2 bonus on saving throws against acid, disease, fire, and poison spells and effects. It also gains an amount of spell resistance equal to 5 + its HD against spells with the good descriptor. The summoner must be evil-aligned to select this evolution.

At 7th level, by spending 2 additional evolution points, the summoner increases the bonus on saving throws to +4 and extends the spell resistance to affect any spells and spell-like abilities cast by good creatures.

At 12th level, by spending 2 additional evolution points, the eidolon gains immunity to acid, disease, fire, and poison. Its spell resistance increases to an amount of equal to 11 + its HD. (The summoner must pay for the 7th-level upgrade before paying for this 12th-level upgrade.)

Evil Spells

The following new spells are useful to those who embrace the forces of darkness in their search for power.

SPELLS WITH THE EVIL DESCRIPTOR

The following spells all have the evil descriptor: *animate dead, blade of dark triumph*UM*, blasphemy, blood transcription*UM*, communal protection from good*UC*, contagion, corruption resistance*APG*, create greater undead, create undead, curse water, cursed earth*UM*, death candle*ARG*, death knell, defile armor*APG*, desecrate, dispel good, dread bolt*UM*, eldritch fever*UM*, enemy's heart*ARG*, epidemic*UM*, excruciating deformation*UM*, fleshworm infestation*UM*, greater contagion*UM*, greater interrogation*UM*, interrogation*UM*, ki leech*UM*, lesser animate dead, magic circle against good, malediction*APG*, mass pain strike*APG*, nightmare, pain strike*APG*, plague carrier*UM*, plague storm*UM*, protection from good, retribution*APG*, sentry skull*ARG*, shadow projection*APG*, symbol of pain, undine's curse*ARG*, unhallow, unholy aura, unholy blight, unholy ice*UM*, unholy sword*UM*, vision of hell*UM*.*

SHARED SUFFERING

School necromancy [evil]; **Level** antipaladin 2, inquisitor 2, sorcerer/wizard 2, witch 2
Casting Time 1 standard action
Components V, F (a silver dagger inlaid with onyx and jade worth 100 gp)
Range long (400 ft. + 40 ft./level)
Target one living creature
Duration instantaneous
Saving Throw none; **Spell Resistance** yes

You infuse a dagger with necromantic energy, then plunge the dagger into your own body. You take 1d6 points of negative energy damage plus 1d6 points of damage for every 2 caster levels you possess beyond 1st (to a maximum of 5d6 at 9th level). The target takes an amount of damage equal to the damage you took this way, plus an amount equal to your Intelligence modifier (if you're a witch or wizard), Wisdom modifier (if you're an inquisitor), or Charisma modifier (if you're an antipaladin or sorcerer).

Damage from this spell cannot be divided by effects such as *shield other* or *unwilling shield*APG; it cuts through such protections completely.

WRACKING RAY

School necromancy [evil, pain]; **Level** sorcerer/wizard 5, witch 5
Casting Time 1 standard action
Components V, M (an old bone, broken in the casting)
Range medium (100 ft. + 10 ft./level)
Effect ray
Duration instantaneous
Saving Throw Fortitude half; **Spell Resistance** yes

A ray of sickly greenish-gray negative energy issues forth from the palm of your hand. Make a ranged touch attack against the target. A creature hit by this spell is wracked by painful spasms as its muscles and sinews wither and twist. The subject takes 1d4 points of Dexterity and Strength damage per 3 caster levels you possess (maximum 5d4 each). This spell cannot reduce an ability score below 1. A successful Fortitude save halves the damage.

UTTER DEPRAVITY

There are those with natures so vile and base needs so dire that little place exists for them in orderly society. While it might seem like this type of person would play poorly with others and fare ill in an adventuring party, even raving lunatics sometimes know they need aid. Whether they're diabolist wizards seeking sacrifices for otherworldly masters, barely sane warriors known for stitching masks from the peeled faces of fallen enemies, or flagellant Kuthite priests believing that all flesh is sculpting matter for their god, such twisted souls still know when to call upon allies or minions for help. The only question for their adventuring companions is whether to overlook these excesses or join in the fun.

ALCHEMICAL WARFARE

Some discoveries should remain undiscovered. The history of alchemy is littered with notes so unethical that many would burn them on sight. There are also those who see such mad conjectures as hypotheses in need of testing.

Alchemist Discoveries

The following alchemist discoveries (see the *Pathfinder RPG Advanced Player's Guide*) are suitable for evil alchemists.

Discoveries that modify bombs and are marked with an asterisk (*) do not stack. Only one such discovery can be applied to an individual bomb. The DC of any saving throw called for by a discovery is equal to 10 + 1/2 the alchemist's class level + the alchemist's Intelligence modifier.

Cursed Bomb*: When an alchemist creates a bomb, he can choose to have it deliver a debilitating curse. A creature that takes a direct hit from a cursed bomb must succeed at a Will save or be affected by *bestow curse*. An alchemist must be at least 12th level to select this discovery.

Pickled Quasit: The alchemist has learned how to seal a quasit in a bottle, which he can prepare for use as an extract. When the alchemist activates the extract, he throws the bottle at a square within 30 feet, releasing the quasit. The quasit is not under the alchemist's control, but is otherwise treated as a summoned creature. The quasit remains for 1 round per caster level, then collapses into its associated elements. If the alchemist has the infusion discovery, another character can use the infused specimen. Creating a pickled quasit requires a 4th-level extract. An alchemist must be at least 10th level to select this discovery.

Plague Vector: The effects of the alchemist's plague bomb operate as normal except for the following changes. The chosen disease's save DC is equal to 10 + 1/2 the alchemist's level + his Intelligence modifier. Any creatures affected by the chosen disease become vectors for it, spreading the disease to any creatures they come in physical contact with for a number of days equal to the alchemist's Intelligence modifier (minimum 1). The save DC to avoid contracting the disease from the vector is the same as the DC used for this discovery. An alchemist must be at least 14th level and must have the plague bomb discovery to select this discovery.

Profane Bomb*: When the alchemist creates a bomb, he can choose to have it deal evil divine damage. Good creatures that take a direct hit from a profane bomb must succeed at a Fortitude save or be staggered on their next turn. Against a neutral creature, a profane bomb deals half damage, and the target is not affected by the bomb's staggering effect. A profane bomb has no effect against evil-aligned creatures. An alchemist must be at least 8th level to select this discovery.

Tainted Infusion: The alchemist can mask murder behind beneficence. When preparing an extract with the infusion discovery, he can lace the extract with one of his bombs as long as the extract has a duration greater than instantaneous. If he chooses, the alchemist can reduce the duration of the extract to 1 round. As soon as the extract's duration expires, it detonates, dealing 150% of the alchemist's bomb damage to the drinker. This effect does not produce a splash radius. Producing a tainted extract consumes both an infusion slot and a daily bomb use. An alchemist must know both the delayed bomb and infusion discoveries to select this discovery.

NEW POISONS

Name	Type	Fort DC	Onset	Frequency	Effect	Cure	Cost
Peasant's woe	Injury	15	—	1/rd. for 4 rds.	–10 ft. speed, 1 Dex	1 save	400 gp
Brain blot	Inhaled	13	1 min.	1/min. for 6 min.	–5 concentration/1 Int	1 save	800 gp
Everwake serum	Ingested	17	—	1/day for 5 days	No sleep; see text	2 saves	2,500 gp

Poisons

The following new types of poisons are popular concoctions among the unscrupulous individuals drawn to such tactics.

BRAIN BLOT

Type poison, inhaled; **Save** Fortitude DC 13
Onset 1 minute; **Frequency** 1/minute for 6 minutes
Initial Effect –5 on concentration checks for 1 hour; **Secondary Effect** 1 Int damage; **Cure** 1 save

EVERWAKE SERUM

Type poison, ingested; **Save** Fortitude DC 16
Frequency 1/day for 5 days
Effect cannot voluntarily rest or sleep (spells such as *sleep* still function as normal), preventing spellcasters who need to rest to regain or prepare spells from doing so; **Cure** 2 saves

PEASANT'S WOE

Type poison, injury; **Save** Fortitude DC 15
Frequency 1/round for 4 rounds
Initial Effect –10 ft. to base speed for 1d6 minutes; **Secondary Effect** 1 Dex damage; **Cure** 1 save

RAGING CANNIBAL (BARBARIAN ARCHETYPE)

While savagery is not inherently evil, some primitive cultures thrive on depravity. The raging cannibal is a barbarian who feasts upon her fallen opponents not out of hunger, or even a taste for flesh, but because she believes physically consuming her foes and defiling their lost lives demonstrates her strength. A raging cannibal has the following class features.

Animal Fury: At 2nd level, a raging cannibal must select animal fury as her first rage power.

Consume Vigor (Ex): At 2nd level, when a raging cannibal reduces a creature of the same creature type as herself to 0 or fewer hit points with her bite attack while raging, she can consume a chunk of its body to gain a portion of its power. When this occurs, the raging cannibal gains 1 additional round of rage, provided the creature's Hit Dice equal or exceed her barbarian level. At 5th level and every 3 levels thereafter, the raging cannibal gains 1 additional round of rage each time this ability is used. This ability replaces uncanny dodge.

Intimidating Gouge (Ex): At 3rd level, when a raging cannibal confirms a critical hit against a creature of the same creature type as herself with her bite attack while raging, she gains a bonus on Intimidate checks equal to half her barbarian level for the duration of the rage. This ability replaces trap sense.

Feed from Fury (Ex): At 5th level, a raging cannibal is empowered by eating her enemies during combat. When a raging cannibal confirms a critical hit against a creature of the same creature type as herself with her bite attack while raging, she gains a number of temporary hit points equal to her barbarian level. These temporary hit points stack with other temporary hit points gained from this ability, but not with those from other sources. These temporary hit points fade after a period of time equal to 10 minutes per barbarian level. This ability replaces improved uncanny dodge.

Razor-Toothed Fury (Ex): At 6th level, a raging cannibal's bite becomes more fearsome. When using her bite attack, the raging cannibal can take a –1 penalty on her attack roll to add 2 points of bleed damage to the damage dealt. At 10th level and every 4 levels thereafter, the attack penalty increases by 1 and the bleed damage increases by 2 points. This ability replaces damage reduction.

Rage Powers: The following rage powers complement the raging cannibal archetype: animal fury, internal fortitude, intimidating glare, primal scentUC, scent, and terrifying howl.

BARBARIAN RAGE POWERS

The following rage powers are appropriate choices for raging cannibals, or any barbarians who like to sink their teeth into their enemies.

Greater Animal Fury (Ex): This power works as animal fury, but the barbarian's bite attack deals damage as if she were one size larger. A barbarian must have the animal fury rage power to select this rage power.

Penetrating Bite (Ex): When using the animal fury rage power while raging, the barbarian's bite is able to pierce most resistances. At 4th level, her bite is treated as a magic weapon for the purpose of overcoming damage reduction. At 7th level, her bite is also treated as cold iron and silver for the purpose of overcoming damage reduction. At 10th level, her bite is also treated as a chaotic weapon for the purpose of overcoming damage reduction. At 16th level, her bite is treated as an adamantine weapon for the purpose of overcoming damage reduction and bypassing hardness. A barbarian must have the animal fury rage power and be at least 4th level to select this rage power.

Savage Jaw (Ex): While raging, the barbarian can open her jaw wide and latch her teeth firmly onto her opponent. While using the animal fury power, the barbarian can activate this power as a free action and gain the grab ability with her bite attack until the start of her next turn. This power can be used only once per rage. A barbarian must have the animal fury rage power to select this rage power.

WICKED AND WEIRD

Evil always shows its true face sooner or later. When banded together with other evil beings, many dark souls proudly display the trappings of their devotion to immoral and hateful acts. Many who embrace evil want to reflect that decision in their appearance, not simply stand out from normal society. Look for true evil among those who revel in showing the world their rotten core by butchering their flesh in devotion to their evil ways or branding their foreheads with their foul deity's symbol.

Nidalese Shadow Piercings

True Nidalese savor pain, and they proudly wear this delight in the torturous piercing of their bodies. Shadow piercers are some of the most skilled pain artisans in Nidal's depraved culture. They create magical pieces of jewelry, formed partially of shadowstuff, and use them in all manner of surface piercings for their discerning clients. Some shadow piercings are more than just single pieces of jewelry—instead they are created in sets that form specific designs across an expanse of the wearer's skin.

Craft Shadow Piercing (Item Creation)

You can craft magical piercings infused with the power of shadow.

Prerequisites: Craft (jewelry) 5 ranks, caster level 5th.

Benefit: You can create special wondrous items—typically barbs, hooks, rings, and spikes—that adorn piercings in the wearer's flesh and grant magical abilities. Both you and the recipient of the piercing (if not yourself) must be present for the entire piercing process.

Shadow piercings must be placed in a part of the body normally associated with a magic item slot, but they do not take up a slot on the body, nor interfere with other magic items that use those slots. A single slot can only hold one shadow piercing (nonmagical piercings do not count against this limit). Shadow piercings can be applied to the following slots: belt, body, chest, eyes, feet, hands, head, neck, shoulder, and wrist.

A single slot can hold multiple physical piercings, though the pieces of jewelry operate as a single item and must be created for that purpose. Shadow piercings have different levels of power: minor, major, and greater. Minor shadow piercings usually include one piece of jewelry, while major and greater shadow piercings often are made up of multiple rings and spikes that cover the entire area of the piercing's slot (but are still considered a single item). A creature can only use a number of shadow piercings equal its Constitution modifier plus its Wisdom modifier.

Carefully inserting or removing a shadow piercing takes a full-round action and deals no damage. Alternatively, a shadow piercing may be pulled out of a creature using the steal maneuver as a standard action that deals 1d6 points of damage. Only a creature with the Craft Shadow Piercing feat may create or insert a shadow piercing, but any creature may remove one. Inserting a shadow piercing is impossible unless the target is willing or helpless. After being removed, a shadow piercing may be inserted into another creature by someone with this feat. Since they are treated as magic items, they are affected by *dispel magic*.

Shadow piercings follow the rules for magic item creation, except the creator can use the Craft (jewelry) skill instead of Spellcraft. New shadow piercings can be researched and designed using the rules for pricing new magic items. Shadow piercing powers for a specific slot must be thematically similar or linked. Since shadow piercings don't interfere with other magic items in the same slot, but can only have one piercing per slot, the base price is multiplied by 1.5 instead of doubled as if they had no space limitation.

BODY PIERCINGS		PRICE varies
Minor		1,800 GP
Major		2,400 GP
Greater		3,200 GP
SLOT body	**CL** 3rd	**WEIGHT** —
AURA faint transmutation		

These piercings come in the form of grotesque spikes and needles that cover every inch of the wearer's skin.

Minor: The wearer gains a +2 competence bonus to CMD against grappling attempts.

Major: Any creature attacking the wearer with a natural or unarmed attack must succeed at a DC 15 Reflex save or take 1d4 points of damage.

Greater: The wearer is considered to have *+1 armor spikes* when not wearing armor or bulky clothing, and is considered proficient with armor spikes.

CONSTRUCTION REQUIREMENTS	COST varies
Minor	900 GP
Major	1,200 GP
Greater	1,600 GP

Craft Shadow Piercing, Improved Grapple, *magic weapon*

CHEST PIERCINGS

CHEST PIERCINGS	PRICE varies
Minor	2,200 GP
Major	3,750 GP
Greater	5,750 GP
SLOT body	**CL** 3rd	**WEIGHT** —
AURA faint transmutation		

These excruciating body ornaments come in the form of sharp barbs and serrated rings inserted in the nipples, abdomen, or along the ribs. The pain they cause sharpens the mind and blocks out distractions.

Minor: The wearer gains a +2 profane bonus on saves against effects that cause the dazed, nauseated, and sickened conditions.

Major: The wearer gains a +5 competence bonus on concentration checks.

Greater: The wearer gains a +4 profane bonus on saving throws against effects that deal ability damage or drain.

CONSTRUCTION REQUIREMENTS	COST varies
Minor	1,100 GP
Major	1,875 GP
Greater	2,875 GP

Craft Shadow Piercing, *bear's endurance* (minor and greater), *fox's cunning* (major)

EYE PIERCINGS

EYE PIERCINGS	PRICE varies
Minor	6,000 GP
Major	18,000 GP
Greater	32,000 GP
SLOT eye	**CL** 5th	**WEIGHT** —
AURA faint transmutation		

These piercings may penetrate the eyebrow, eyelid, or the eye itself. Due to magical, they do not impair the owner's vision. All effects from an eye piercing are continuous.

Minor: The wearer gains low-light vision. If the wearer already has low-light vision, the ability's range is doubled.

Major: The wearer gains darkvision to 60 feet.

Greater: The wearer gains the see in darkness special ability.

CONSTRUCTION REQUIREMENTS	COST varies
Minor	3,000 GP
Major	9,000 GP
Greater	16,000 GP

Craft Shadow Piercing, *keen senses*[APG] (minor), *darkvision* (major and greater)

HEAD PIERCINGS

HEAD PIERCINGS	PRICE varies
Minor	3,750 GP
Major	6,000 GP
Greater	33,600 GP
SLOT head	**CL** 5th	**WEIGHT** —
AURA faint transmutation		

Whether they are crowns of pins, pinned-back lips, or simple nose rings, these piercings accentuate the owner's terrifying presence and inner resolve.

Minor: The wearer gains a +5 competence bonus on Intimidate checks.

Major: The wearer gains a +4 profane bonus against mind-affecting effects.

Greater: The wearer can use *fear* twice per day (Will DC 16).

CONSTRUCTION REQUIREMENTS	COST varies
Minor	1,875 GP
Major	3,000 GP
Greater	16,800 GP

Craft Shadow Piercing, *fear* (minor and greater), *owl's wisdom* (major)

SUSPENSION PIERCINGS

SUSPENSION PIERCINGS	PRICE varies
Minor	6,000 GP
Major	7,200 GP
Greater	11,200 GP
SLOT belt or shoulder	**CL** 7th	**WEIGHT** —
AURA faint transmutation (minor and major), moderate transmutation (greater)		

These piercings are popular among suspensionists, who hang from hooks attached to their skin.

Minor: The wearer gains *feather fall* as a continuous effect.

Major: The wearer may use *levitate* twice per day.

Greater: The wearer may use *air walk* once per day.

CONSTRUCTION REQUIREMENTS	COST varies
Minor	3,000 GP
Major	3,600 GP
Greater	5,600 GP

Craft Shadow Piercing, *feather fall* (lesser), *levitate* (normal), *air walk* (greater)

DRAWBACKS

Being evil in a decent society isn't easy, and keeping true to your dark soul can be a complicated business. More information on drawbacks can be found in *Pathfinder RPG Ultimate Campaign*.

Foul Brand: You have the symbol of an evil deity burned into your flesh. If the symbol is on your hand, you take a –1 penalty on Disable Device, Disguise, and Sleight of Hand checks. If the symbol is on your face, you take a –2 penalty on Bluff, Diplomacy, and Disguise checks. This does not count as a holy symbol for the purposes of a divine focus for spellcasting.

Umbral Unmasking: You cast no shadow whatsoever, or the shadow you do have is monstrous. Under normal lighted conditions, this is not hard to observe—but uncommon to notice. Creatures that succeed at a DC 15 Wisdom check notice it plainly (an additional Perception check may be required based on environmental conditions). This telltale sign of wickedness cannot be concealed by *misdirection*, *nondetection*, or illusions, except those that also affect shadows (such as *invisibility*).

Warded Against Nature: Animals do not willingly approach within 30 feet of you, unless you or the animal's master succeeds at a DC 20 Handle Animal, Ride, or wild empathy check. Animal companions, familiars, and mounts granted by your class abilities are immune to this effect.

MAGIC ITEMS

Champions of corruption tend to make use of magic items that allow them to profit at others' expense, punish those who dare oppose their foul plans, or draw upon new types of evil magic.

AMULET OF EUPHORIC HEALING		PRICE 12,000 GP
SLOT neck	CL 3rd	WEIGHT 1 lb.
AURA faint enchantment		

These glass amulets hold bubbling red liquid and often feature a religion's or deity's holy symbol, most commonly that of Asmodeus or Zon-Kuthon. While worn, the amulet tinges the user's healing magic with a wash of ecstasy that acts as a magical drug, making the recipient of the magical healing susceptible to mental manipulation by the wearer. Anytime the wearer casts a healing spell or uses a spell-like ability on a single target, the recipient of the magical healing additionally must succeed at a DC 13 Fortitude save or become addicted to the wearer's healing spells. The wearer can suppress this effect by shielding the amulet from view with a hand or held item as a free action. The drug has the following statistics.

EUPHORIC HEALING

Type spell **Addiction** minor, Fortitude DC 13
Effect 24 hours, –2 penalty against all mind-affecting spells cast by the amulet's wearer
Damage 1 Wis damage

CONSTRUCTION REQUIREMENTS	COST 6,000 GP
Craft Wondrous Item, *cure light wounds, enthrall*	

COLLAR OF UNLIVING SERVITUDE		PRICE 14,000 GP
SLOT neck	CL 7th	WEIGHT 1 lb.
AURA moderate necromancy		

This black iron choker chain forges a link between the wearer and any undead creature of the wearer's choice. Creating this link requires a command word. The wearer can dismiss this bond with another command word, and reforge it with the same or a different undead creature at a later time. While the two are bound and within 100 feet of one another, any positive energy damage the undead would take is instead transferred to the wearer as healing. Likewise, any negative energy damage the wearer would take transfers to and heals the undead. The collar can transfer up to 70 total points of damage per day.

CONSTRUCTION REQUIREMENTS	COST 7,000 GP
Craft Wondrous Item, *shield other* or *unwilling shield*APG	

DARK LIFE RING		PRICE 1,250 GP
SLOT ring	CL 3rd	WEIGHT —
AURA faint necromancy		

Mortal blacksmiths residing in the Gebbite city of Graydirge created the first *dark life rings*. Too often had these living unfortunates suffered collateral damage from the negative energy effects used daily in the streets of the undead-ruled city, so they forged these rings in hopes of mitigating at least some of the harm their unliving rulers carelessly inflicted upon them. Before the Blood Lords at Mechitar could punish the insolent smiths of Graydirge, the *dark life rings* and their imitators made their way into the wider world.

A *dark life ring* grants its wearer a +2 profane bonus on Will saving throws against channeled negative energy and inflict spells (any spell with "inflict" in its name). In addition, anytime the wearer takes damage from channeled negative energy or an inflict spell, she subtracts 5 from the damage taken (calculated after the wearer has rolled her Will save against the effect), to a minimum of 0 points of damage.

CONSTRUCTION REQUIREMENTS	COST 625 GP
Forge Ring, *death ward*	

DIRGESINGER'S CHOIR		PRICE 34,000 GP
SLOT none	CL 13th	WEIGHT 3 lbs.
AURA strong necromancy [evil]		

Equal parts grisly and lovely, this unusual harp-like musical instrument is crafted from a corpse, with a bone frame, skin stretched around the soundbox for percussion, and strings of twisted hair. When played, it can summon forth a soul bound to it. Initially, the soul is that of the person whose corpse was used to make the instrument. The spirit manifests in an adjacent square as a translucent, intangible image of the person as he was in life. The image cannot attack or be attacked in any way. It is clearly distressed by the musician's playing; it wails an eerie, pained accompaniment that nonetheless enhances the music's quality, granting a +4 circumstance bonus on Performance checks made with the instrument and (if the performer is a bard) adding 1 to the DC of a dirge of doom, frightening tune, or deadly performance played on the instrument.

If an undead is within 30 feet, the musician can command the bound soul to seize it as a standard action. The undead must attempt a DC 20 Will save. If it's successful, the image dissipates for 1 day; if it fails, the soul rides the undead for 1d4+1 rounds, acting as *control undead* cast by the musician. If the musician has the bardic performance ability, she can continue playing and spend a round of bardic performance as a free action each round to prevent that round from counting toward the duration of this effect. The soul dissipates for 1 day after the effect ends.

Crafting the instrument destroys the original body; that creature cannot be brought back to life via *raise dead*. As long as the instrument exists, *resurrection* and *true resurrection* can revive the creature only if they're cast on the instrument itself; doing so destroys the instrument. The instrument cannot be affected by spells that target corpses, such as *animate dead* or *decompose corpse*^{UM}.

CONSTRUCTION REQUIREMENTS	COST 17,000 GP

Craft Wondrous Item, *control undead, ghost sound*, creator must be evil

ELIXIR OF REPRESSION	PRICE 150 GP
SLOT none	CL 3rd	WEIGHT —
AURA faint enchantment		

A draught of this pale blue liquid imposes a dull placidity upon the imbiber, making him less quick to anger while not significantly impairing his mental functions. A drinker with homicidal or other antisocial tendencies can dull his more extreme urges with regular doses of this elixir, allowing him to blend into society without resorting to murder, assault, or other actions that might make day-to-day life difficult. Additionally, the elixir gives the imbiber a +2 insight bonus on saving throws against any mind-affecting spell or effect. As a side effect, the imbiber must succeed at a DC 13 Will save to benefit from spells and effects that grant a morale bonus. An imbiber who is afflicted with any form of madness receives a +4 insight bonus on any saving throws made to resist the effects of that madness during the elixir's duration. A dose of elixir of repression lasts for 12 hours.

CONSTRUCTION REQUIREMENTS	COST 75 GP

Craft Wondrous Item, *calm emotions*

HAND OF HOARDED DEATHS	PRICE 25,000 GP
SLOT hand	CL 7th	WEIGHT —
AURA moderate necromancy		

The wearer of this single, black silk glove can use *death knell* on command. The target of *death knell* dies if it fails a DC 13 Fortitude save as normal, but the glove's wearer does not immediately benefit from the death; instead the siphoned life energy is stored inside the glove. The glove indefinitely holds a reservoir of up to five deaths. The wearer can tap into these deaths anytime thereafter by touching herself with the glove as a swift action, granting her *death knell*'s benefits with a duration of 10 minutes. She can spend more than one death at a time, if she wishes. Temporary hit points from multiple deaths stack, but the bonuses to caster level and Strength do not. If multiple deaths are spent at the same time, add their durations together.

CONSTRUCTION REQUIREMENTS	COST 12,500 GP

Craft Wondrous Item, *death knell, false life*

RING OF PLAGUES	PRICE 20,000 GP
SLOT ring	CL 11th	WEIGHT —
AURA moderate necromancy		

This silver ring is set with a black opal. Once per day, when the wearer is reduced to half or fewer of her maximum hit point total, whoever dealt the activating blow to the wearer is immediately subjected to a *major curse*^{UM} with unlimited range. A successful DC 19 Will saving throw is needed to negate the spell. Rather than one of the listed curse effects, the curse imposes a −4 penalty on the victim's saving throws and causes the victim to contract a disease chosen by the wearer from the contagion list without a save. The cursed disease has no onset time, but the attacker is allowed the normal saving throw to avoid its effects. It can be cured only by successfully casting both *remove curse* and *remove disease* within 1 minute of each other. Those exposed to the cursed attacker thereafter must save against the mundane version of the disease or become infected (though they are not cursed).

Once per day, if the wearer is killed or reduced to negative hit points, a plague of curses is unleashed. The attacker and the attacker's five nearest allies or immediate blood relatives become the targets of the curse described above. If the wearer is restored to at least 1 hit point, these curses end, allowing surviving victims to recover naturally.

CONSTRUCTION REQUIREMENTS	COST 10,000 GP

Forge Ring, *contagion, major curse*^{UM}, *spite*^{APG}

SINNER'S WAGE	PRICE 500 GP
SLOT none	CL 7th	WEIGHT —
AURA moderate enchantment		

A *sinner's wage* is a round golden coin with two blank faces. When placed among nonmagical currency, it adopts the size, shape, and any embellishments (such as an engraving or stamp) of the majority of the other coins.

When included as payment for any service that compromises the recipient's morals (such as a bribe for a lawful city guard to look the other way, or a contribution to a good politician to pass dubious legislation), a *sinner's wage* makes the offered payment more tempting. The giver of the *sinner's wage* gains a +2 profane bonus on Charisma checks and Bluff, Diplomacy, and Intimidate checks to convince the recipient to perform the service in question. Thus, the item can be used to pay off a guard as well as convince an outsider to perform a service with a *planar binding* spell (in the latter case, the +2 profane bonus stacks with the bonus normally granted for offering a reward to the outsider).

In addition, a *sinner's wage* can be used as an optional focus component when the owner casts any charm or compulsion spell of 5th level or lower. When a creature is subject to a spell incorporating this focus, it takes a −2 penalty on all rolls to resist acting against its nature (whether a Will saving throw or a Charisma check). Using the *sinner's wage* in this fashion temporarily drains the magic from the coin, rendering it unusable for any purpose for a period of 1 week.

CONSTRUCTION REQUIREMENTS	COST 250 GP

Craft Wondrous Item, *charm monster*

Next Month!

Bring the 10 new classes from the *Pathfinder RPG Advanced Class Guide* to life with *Pathfinder Player Companion: Advanced Class Origins*! With all-new archetypes, traits, feats, magic items, spells, and more, this volume is the ultimate resource for bloodragers and warpriests alike. Whether you're making a swashbuckler from the Shackles or a skald from the Lands of the Linnorm Kings, *Advanced Class Origins* lets you delve into the powers of Golarion's most iconic cultures and groups in countless new ways!

Would you like to know more?

Having thoroughly steeped your antihero in the corruption explored throughout this volume, it would be foolish to believe that your quest for unholy power stops here. Check out the following Pathfinder RPG books to turn your villain into a true force of reckoning.

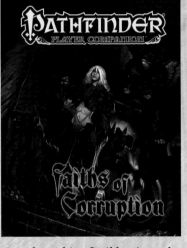

Casual worship of evil has its perks, but only the most devout can hope to glean true powers of wickedness from their foul deities. Become a paragon of evil with *Pathfinder Player Companion: Faiths of Corruption*.

What is a champion of corruption without a fiend to guide her vile ways? Find details on the devils, demons, and worse that rule the evil Outer Planes with the *Pathfinder Campaign Setting: Books of the Damned* series.

Devote yourself wholly to the path of evil and marvel at the powers you wield. Inherit the might of Blackfire Adepts, Daggermark poisoners, or Umbral Court agents with *Pathfinder Campaign Setting: Paths of Prestige*.